Searching for God

Francis L. Gross, Jr.

Sheed & Ward

Grateful acknowledgment is made to the following
for permission to reprint:

Excerpt from *The Color Purple,* copyright© 1982 by Alice Walker, reprinted by permission of Harcourt Brace Jovanovich, Inc.

"i thank You God for most this amazing" is reprinted from XAIPE by E. E. Cummings, Edited by George James Firmage, by permission of Liveright Publishing Corporation. Copyright© 1950 by E. E. Cummings. Copyright© 1979, 1978, 1973 by Nancy T. Andrews. Copyright© 1979, 1973 by George James Firmage.

Lawrence Ferlinghetti: *A Coney Island of the Mind.* Copyright© 1958 by Lawrence Ferlinghetti. Reprinted by permission of New Directions Publishing Corporation.

Sheed & Ward™ is a service of National Catholic Reporter Publishing Company, Inc.

Library of Congress Catalog Card Number: 89-61928

ISBN: 1-55612-274-8

Published by: Sheed & Ward
                 115 E. Armour Blvd. P.O. Box 419492
                 Kansas City, MO 64141-6492

To order, call: (800) 333-7373

Contents

With affection,
to the undergraduates
of Western Michigan University

Acknowledgements

This book owes a great deal to a number of figures in the field of developmental psychology. Erik Erikson's celebrated eight stages of the life cycle is a firm foundation. Rogert Kegan's stages as put forth in *The Developing Self* (Harvard, 1982) underlies much of my comments on how children and adolescents think. James W. Fowler's work on faith development has been both an inspiration and a guide. Lawrence Kohlberg, whose death has saddened me this year, is so much a seminal thinker to these pages that I cannot begin to assign him a definite place. Carol Gilligan, Mary Belenky and her associates and Nancy Chodorow have helped me understand women's ways of understanding and believing.

Conversations with Dr. Richard Shulik and my wife, Dr. Toni Perior Gross, have helped tie my observations closer to the realities of real people.

Sigmund Freud, C.G. Jung and Jean Piaget are the grandfathers of this work, whether they like it or not.

Francis L. Gross, Jr.
Western Michigan University
April 15, 1989

Foreword

The title of this book might just as well be simply *Searching For God*. Frank Gross would add "in college" because that is where he works and because he has a love for honest searchers rooted deeply in his tough-tender teacher's heart. Gross's searchers—like today's college students—can come in any age category. Through Gross's sprightly prose and playful imagery, it becomes clear that he knows and loves God. In a *genre* similar to *Everything I Needed To Know I Learned in Kindergarten*, Gross's book invites the reader to an engaging journey of imagination and encounter.

But there is more. The ease and pace of his prose cannot conceal the fact that Gross has been a careful student of the psychology of human development. With a verve I find endearing he has taken the perspectives of Jean Piget, Lawrence Kohlberg, Robert Kegan, Carol Gilligan, and my own work in faith developement, and made them lucidly accessible. Through stories—his own and those of others—he invites readers of all ages to reflect upon the experiences of their unfolding lives. He alerts us to look for the threads of transcendence woven into the events and relations that make up the tapestries of our lives.

The musings that make up this book have been tried and tested on the most demanding of audiences. Undergraduate students do not pretend interest. There is nothing more discouraging than forty pairs of eyes in a classroom going glassy at the same time. Achieving an unusual blend of intellectual integrity and a well-honed communicator's genius, Frank Gross offers a text which will serve as a lively introduction to theology as well as to the developmental psychology of religion. I commend it to teachers and other searchers with enthusiasm.

James W. Fowler
Emory University

v

The perception of the divine omnipresence is essentially a seeing, a taste, that is to say a sort of intuition bearing upon certain superior qualities in things. It cannot, therefore, be attained directly by any process of reasoning, nor by any human artifice. It is a gift, like life itself, of which it is undoubtedly the supreme experimental perfection.

—Pierre Teilhard de Chardin

I do believe that feeling is the deeper source of religion, and that philosophic and theological formulas are secondary products, like translations of a text into another tongue.

—William James

Pierre Teilhard de Chardin, *The Divine Milieu* (New York: Harper and Row, 1960), p. 131.

William James, *The Varieties of Religious Experience* (New York: Modern Library, 1902), p. 422.

1

Honesty and the Search

This book is for people who are confused. As the title indicates, it is about people who are confused about God. I want you to know right now that my concern as author of the book is not to get you to join any particular church or tradition. I'm concerned with your making a good decision. To be frank, I myself believe that there are a number of good religious traditions. I simply don't believe that any one of them has the lion's share of the truth, certainly not all of the truth. The fact that I am a Roman Catholic does not mean that I think you should be one. I by no means believe that my version of Christianity is the best one or that Christianity is the best of world religions.

The Christian tradition is the one I was born into; my roots are there. Within the Christian spectrum of churches I was also born into Roman Catholicism. I'm glad to be there, not because I think we are the best, but because I have found a home in my church. Not only was I born there, but as a young adult I decided it was a good place to be and elected to stay with the church of my roots. It is a good place for me, but it might well not be a good place for you.

When I said that this book is for people who are confused, I meant it. I am taking for granted that as a college student you are no longer as sure about the God and church of your childhood as you once were. You may have grown up in a godless or churchless tradition. If you did, I am assuming that you are questioning that. If you are perfectly at home with your God and your religion, don't read this book. If you are just fine without any God or without any church, I don't have much to say to you. Unless it be to express my hope that somewhere along the line you do question your god-beliefs and your church, even if it is the church of nowhere. I think that you can never be an adult person, *whether religious or nonreligious*, until you have tested the tradition you have come from and tried to come to terms with what you are going to do about it in the future.

Surely one of the main purposes of going to college in the first place is to learn new ideas as well as questioning old ones. But I heartily believe that your religious knowledge and practice should be just as adult as your knowledge of your college major. It distresses me, and I hope it distresses you, to talk to someone who has a very subtle knowledge of engineering or business but who sees no reason for deep or subtle knowledge of religious issues. You can talk engineering or business on an adult level, but when it comes to religion you have to shift gears and use the language of a child. I can see no reason why a person has to turn in her head in order to be religious. The first book of the Hebrew scriptures[1] says that human beings are made in the image and likeness of God. Our intelligences and intuitions are reflections of the divine in most religious traditions. My presumption is that any educated person will apply as best she can her own intelligence in her search for God.

This is another way of saying that I don't think anyone need fear being honest in the search for religious truth. I don't know of a great religious tradition that tolerates telling lies. Preachers, priests, or rabbis who tell their people just to read their holy books and ask no questions are surely asking for stupidity and dishonesty. Do you see what I am getting at? It is not uncommon for a person to think it is wrong to question his tradition. In Catholic parlance, you wouldn't question your beliefs for fear of "losing your faith." And of course, if you lose your faith, the jaws of hell are open wide to receive you when you die.

I grant you that if you question things, you may change your mind. That's what questioning is all about. If you question God or your church, you may never again believe in God with the simplicity of a child, and you may decide that you don't want to stay in your own church, or even that God is an illusion. At the same time, if you do *not* question your faith, your religion—or the lack of it—will remain childish and superstitious all your life long. That's not just a risk; it's a sure thing. I'm proposing the risk as the only sensible way to go.

College years are especially fruitful times to question for a number of reasons. If you have just left high school, home, and family, you are experiencing for the first time a much wider world than the world of home. It is perfectly normal to need to experiment with a lot of things as you try to find yourself in this wider and more adult arena. Developmental psychologists call the teen years and the twenties the years of the Identity Crisis.[2] During the crisis of identity it is quite normal for a person to ask two very basic questions: "What have I got?" and "What am I going to do with it?" One of the things you have "got" from your childhood is a religious tradition or a secular tradition of values. What you are going to do with it is your task as well as the subject matter of this book.

I want to note in passing that I am well aware that undergraduate students are not all fresh out of high school in their late teens. Some of you are older, coming back to college for reasons of your own. I offer you older ones this comment. Although you may be well beyond the years of the identity crisis, it may be that you have some religious questions that have pestered you down the years. It may be that your own teens or twenties came and went very fast. For example, if you married when you were twenty-two and had perforce to go to work, there might well be some unfinished business left over from a crisis of identity that never really had time to come to a conclusion.[3] There are plenty of other times in the human life cycle for taking a second look at values and commitments. One of the most basic purposes of the undergraduate years is to take that second, or third, or fourth look, no matter what your age. Put in a nutshell, you can be confused at any age. Don't rule yourself out of this book because you are an older, "nontraditional" student.

So, we are taking for granted that the university provides a sort of haven for questioners. It is a good place for suspending old judgments and trying on new ones. As a professor, I know that all universities put a high premium on solving questions in an intellectual way. Universities are places for making head trips. As students, you know that there are many other kinds of trips besides intellectual ones. You can get into sports, romantic relationships, all kinds of other friendships. Food can be a trip; so can drinking, and dancing and acting crazy and having a good time—just generally living it up. There are lots of life-expanding experiments in college other than merely intellectual ones. You can't learn everything out of a book.

It is my conviction that you can't learn all that much about the beginnings of an adult knowledge of God or a religious tradition from a book or in a class. You can learn some things from reading, but the rock bottom of the search for God is not just theory. Religion cuts much deeper than the world of mere reason.

Let's use an analogy. You can't learn to make friends out of a book. You can't think your way into a friendship. Making friends is a mysterious activity that involves going out and meeting people. It involves being attracted to some people and not others. It involves being generous and being brave and being faithful. You have to go out of your room; you have to take the risk of meeting other people. And then, of course, you have to wait to see if it will happen. Being receptive is just as important in making friends as being aggressive. Making friends is a very intuitive process; reason and logic often do not play the most important role. Let me remind you that reason and logic are the main things taught at universities. Making friends is something you have to learn on your own, outside of class. I want to suggest to you here that the search for a meaningful God is not primarily a matter of reason any more than making friends is. Attraction, sensitivity, and hunches are important. Proving the existence of God is not much more useful in searching for God than a book on the philosophy of friendship is in making friends. There is a place for logic and theory in both the activities we are describing, but it is a secondary place.[4]

When I get to know a friend, the process is quite different than getting to know accounting or English grammar or computer theory. Knowing a person is different from knowing a book. You have to *meet* friends; you have to bump into them; feelings are important in friendship.

Feelings are important in a search for God too. Your task is to find some way of meeting this mysterious person. It's not made any easier when you realize that you are trying to meet someone you cannot see and whose existence you may not be sure of. You and I both know that ministers, priests, and rabbis sometimes make this meeting harder rather than easier, because clergy often know before they talk to you just what they want to happen. Talking to a clergyperson can be like talking to a car dealer. The car dealer wants you to buy one of *his cars*. He usually does not want you to buy the best car for you, especially if that car is on somebody else's lot. Not all clergy are that way, but it *is* an occupational disease. Maybe you know what I mean from your own experience.

We have established, then, that you are concerned with taking a second look at whatever religious or moral commitment you learned as a child. I have suggested that such a task goes far beyond the world of reason. In a search for God and religion the parallel of making a friend is an apt one. We are dealing with a matter of personal contact. There we hit an obstacle, simple but formidable. How to attempt contact? You are familiar with the process of making friends. You have to be available and willing, and of course, you have to wait. You have to give friendship time to form. It's as though you hang around a person to whom you have been attracted to see if something further will occur. There is an element in making friends that carries with it a certain mystery. You can handle the preliminaries, but after they are over, something else happens or does not happen which neither of the two persons involved have much control over except for remaining receptive to whatever happens.

It is as though the friendship has a life of its own apart from the two people involved. Prospective friends have to give that life a chance to grow or wither, but they cannot make the process happen. You have made friends yourself; I'm sure you are aware of the process. It is often exasperating, because friendships do have a way of turning out quite differently from the plans so carefully laid by people trying to make friends.

This is familiar matter to all of us, no matter how exasperating. What is less familiar is the process of making friends with a person who transcends material reality, who cannot be seen and who does not speak to us the way our human friends do. I don't want to make this process overly mysterious, because people have been making contact with God as far back as history goes. They do it by one form or other of prayer. That is the word used for the process. It is at the heart of all religious traditions. Without it, all the theorizing about God is dust and ashes. Prayer is the word used for contact. If you are serious in your search for God, then a good, hard look at the nature of prayer is called for.

You remember that in order to make friends, a person has to listen to another person, besides talking to that other. A person has to be in the other one's company and to wait for something to develop. The language of prayer is like that. There's some talking, a lot of listening, and a great deal of waiting to see what will develop. Prayer is an art, just as making friends is an art. Please be patient with me; it may seem to you that this explanation is going awfully slow. But, you see, I can't say everything all at once. Besides, being in an area where most modern Americans are primitives, we really don't know much about it.[5]

In order to explain what I mean, I want to go back with you into your own past, to the days of your childhood. There, I want to help you remember how you yourself first learned to pray as a child. Childhood contains the roots of where you are now. Since you are no longer a child, you can look back at those days with some distance; you can learn from those days. So let's take a look at how children learn this activity so vital to contact with the deity. That is the subject of our next chapter.

Notes

[1]Genesis 1:26.

[2]The term "Crisis of Identity" was coined by Erik H. Erikson. He describes it in many places, but never better than in his first book,

Childhood and Society (New York: W.W. Norton, 1963, Revised edition), Chapter Seven. pp. 261-63. See also *Identity: Youth and Crisis* (New York: Norton, 1968), Chapter IV, pp. 179-188.

[3]Erik Erikson is useful here also. He sees clearly that among some kinds of people the crisis of identity can reoccur later in life. Cf. *Identity: Youth and Crisis*, Chapter IV, p. 196-207.

[4]I refer the reader to the Postscript of this book.

[5]C.G. Jung describes the learning of our times as follows: "The marvelous development of science and technics is counterbalanced by an appalling lack of wisdom and introspection." *Psychology and Religion* (New Haven: Yale Press, 1938), p. 18-19.

2

Childhood's Prayer

Developmental psychologists tell us that the years of childhood, when one is beyond infancy and the age of being a toddler, are very businesslike years.1 These years have been termed the years of "being in business for yourself." Think of yourself as a kid running a lemonade stand. One cent for a paper cup full. Think of Lucy's stand in the comic strip *Peanuts* where she charges a penny for psychological advice. Think of writing letters to Santa Claus. Your idea of fairness was tied up in the idea that "a fair exchange is no robbery." In order to get something, you must give something. Your prayers followed this paradigm pretty well too.

When you decided to contact the Almighty One, it was almost always with a request.[6] Oftentimes children have a sort of litany they say before going to bed, "God bless Mom and Dad, my sister Lucy, my brother Joe, all my aunts and uncles." You pray for the people you need for your own life with real fervor. And you figure that if you go to the trouble to ask God to protect them, then God will do just that. You ask God for all sorts of things for yourself, supported perhaps with a text from the Bible or other holy book. After all, the Bible says, "Seek and you shall find, knock and it shall be opened to you." You figure that if you do your part by asking, then God will have to do God's part by responding to your request. Fair is fair, after all. You probably got some shocks when you asked for something, like a new bike at Christmas time and didn't get it. If you didn't get it, your sense of fairness was outraged. Here are a couple of samples taken from letters children have written to God.[2]

Dear God,

I wrote you before do you remember? Well I did what I promised. But you did not send me the horse yet. What about it?

—Lewis

Dear God,

Why can't you even keep it from raining on Saturday all the time?

—Rose

Dear God,

If you do all these things you are pretty busy. Now here's my question. When is the best time I can talk to you. I know you are always listening but when will you be listening hard in Troy, New York.

—Sincerely yours
Allen

Dear God,

I got left back, Thanks a lot.

—Raymond

I'm sure you get the general idea; you may well have some memories of childhood prayers of your own.

Another thing about your childhood. It was populated with only two kinds of people, good guys and bad guys. Kids think in black and white terms. If you aren't one of us, you are one of them. We are good, of course, and they are bad. In the simple world of childhood generally speaking, my family and I are good guys; the members of my church are good guys; my God is a good guy; my friends are good guys. Everybody else is a bad guy, and once in a while I decide my sister Susie is a bad guy, or my father, or the rabbi. There's no middle ground in childhood. He who is not with me is against me. That's that; subtleties come later.

The world of childhood does not understand the religious injunction, "Pray for your enemies." If you do pray for your enemies, it's because your mother or dad will get mad if you don't. Sometimes, even God becomes an enemy, a bad guy, if you don't get the bicycle you asked for for Christmas. Only in later years, beginning in college do you begin to see that there are gray areas in life. Some people are partly good and partly bad. Some questions have more than one right answer. Some of those who are not my own people are decent people.

Your prayers, for the most part, were formulas which you learned to recite. The ones that meant the most to you were all forms of requests for things or people you cared about. You learned those formulas from your family or church and said them at the times your family or church picked out. You prayed before bed, before meals, in church on Sundays or in the temple on Saturdays, and in times of need. You learned as well the proper places for prayer—your bedside or at your mother's knee, in temple or church or mosque. Perhaps what is most important in all this is that you didn't question how and where and when to pray. You just learned and did. Monkey see, monkey do. I don't mean to say that there was no meaning there, but I do mean to say that the meaning was pretty much centered around your own material needs and that you did your praying the way you learned it.

What kind of a person was your God when you were a child? God was a person very much like your parents. One who rewards good and punishes evil the same way your family did, except from a higher throne. In order to get something from God, you had to come up with a price. You certainly had to ask politely . . . or if you found that nagging was effective with your human parents, very likely you nagged God too. You took the stories in your tradition that concerned God very seriously and very literally. If Jesus said, "Ask the father anything in my name and he will give it to you," that's what you did. When it didn't work, you figured maybe you didn't say it right or maybe that God was busy doing something else.

I should like to add something to the very pragmatic approach to God that characterizes most children. There is definitely something more.

Many children have a sense of wonder and awe that they lose in later years.[3] The world is a marvelous place to them. A child can spend a long time looking out the window or playing with simple blocks. A child can use a cardboard box as a make-believe house for hours and hours at a time.

That sense of marveling is frequently a part of a child's notion of God. For God to be mysterious and awe inspiring is second nature for a child. There was a time in your life when it was second nature to you and to me. The poet that lives in almost every child is often difficult to keep alive in later years. If that sense dies altogether, one very important avenue for searching out God dies with it.

So, the prayers of your childhood were rather unreflective pleas for things you wanted. They were quite businesslike. You did your part and you expected God to do his, or hers. You regarded God as a parentlike figure who must be properly buttered up to get good results in your bargaining. God was moreover possessed of an aura of mystery and wonder that came quite naturally to you as a child. Your approach to this mysterious one was quite conventional and unquestioned. It was what you learned at home or in your church.

I have wanted to review this with you, because with the advent of puberty and the onset of the crisis of identity, only the remnants of your childhood prayers stayed with you if your religious life began to stretch and grow the way your body did and the way your mind did in high school and college. There were a lot of changes in your life which inevitably changed your approach to God. In the chapter coming up we will talk about those changes.

Notes

[1] Robert Kegan describes this time in life as "The Imperial Self." It is he who coined the phrase "being in business for yourself." Cf. *The Evolving Self* (Cambridge: Harvard Press, 1982), pp. 89-95. James Fowler is an excellent reference here too. He describes the faith life of children as very practical, concerned with stories, and linear in its think-

ing. Cf. *Stages of Faith* (New York: Harper and Row, 1981), pp. 135-150.

[2]*Children's Letters to God* compiled by Eric Marshall and Stuart Hample (New York: Simon and Schuster, 1966). Nearly all the letters illustrate the point I am here making.

[3]James Fowler is very helpful describing this sense of wonder in very young children. Cf. *Stages of Faith*, pp. 122-124.

3

Youth's Prayer

Youth is the period in a person's life between childhood and adulthood. It begins with the onset of puberty and ends at various times for various people. As a general rule of thumb we can say that it generally ends in one's late twenties. It ends at whatever time one gets a good hold on those two questions I mentioned in an earlier chapter: "What have I got?" and "What am I going to do with it?" I don't mean to say that there is no room for growth and change in adult life, but there are usually some fundamental options taken in your youthful years that forever affect whatever you do with your life later. Youth is a major crossroads in anybody's life. It is the time of the crisis of identity.[1]

Well, what are the changes? Certainly one common one is the development of a newfound sense of loyalty to friends and family.[2] It's true that little kids stick by family and friends, but the little people, you will recall are mainly in business for themselves. The change I am talking about has to do with a less selfish bond, where you stick by your buddies even if it costs you. If a whole classroom of junior high kids is kept in after school until one person confesses to having written "Shit" on the chalk board, sometimes no one will tell on the culprit even though all the students in the room know who did it. That loyalty is partly built on a newfound ability to think about the feelings of other people. You begin to learn to walk in somebody else's shoes. There is really a beautiful generosity about those early friendships and family ties. You never forget them. The fierce loyalty of those years is the subject of many a story, many a song, many a film. Remember the movie *Stand By Me*, and the song by the same title? I might add that there is a real strain

13

when the people you are loyal to have different values. Suppose your family wants you to be home at eleven o'clock and your friends want to stay out until two. That's a bind.

The whole idea of being and acting cool is tied to loyalty to friends. In the years when you first discovered friends, you expressed that bond by acting and dressing just like your buddies, or the people you wished were your buddies—the "in" crowd. You can look back on those days now with amusement. You can see your younger brothers and sisters dressing in all kinds of outlandish ways because that's how the people they admire dress. These are the years when you begin to discover that your parents are people. When you were little, your mother could have been called Lunch or Breakfast, or Cookie or Money, because you saw her as a provider. Now, something funny happens, she's a person. Sometimes you feel for her just as sometimes you feel for your friends. The bond between you and your mother can grow much deeper now.

I think the same thing is true of God. The God of your childhood was Superlunch or Superbreakfast or Supercookie or Supergift. This is a time when you are able for the first time to use the word "person" for God and mean it. If you are a part of the Christian tradition, this is a time when you might be really blown away by getting to know the person of the Jesus of the gospels. You put yourself in his shoes, trying to imagine his thoughts and feelings all those years ago in the mountains and dusty roads of Galilee and Judea.

If you are Jewish, you might discover for the first time the personhood of Abraham or Moses or Elijah—or Judith or Ruth or Esther. The great heroes of your tradition are able to appear to you in a new light altogether and with a new loyalty. Just as your friends inspire you, so can the great people of your tradition inspire you.

Mind you, I am fully aware that along with the possibility of a religious awakening born of your new found affinity for loyalty to friends, so also you have a new found ability to question. You can think about the values you have received in your childhood and wonder for the first time if they are true or useful. It's almost like saying that when you discover that your father is a man like other men, with feelings, with good days and bad days, with good ideas and bad ideas, THEN you realize that it's very possible that some of the things he and your mother taught you are not true. What a bummer! It's exciting to have the freedom to think things over for yourself, but it's scary too.

Sooner or later the issue of God and church will come up for review. Maybe for the first time in your life you consider that there might be something to the idea of God, even though your family doesn't find such a thing meaningful. Maybe you do just the opposite. Your family are all church going Baptists . . . and you begin to wonder about all the hypocrites you see in church . . . people who pretend to be pious but who are well known around town as not practicing what they profess on Sundays.

In any case, along with the discovery of a new dimension in God and the holy people of your tradition, comes the ability and even the need to question the whole business. You don't ask for those questions; they just come. They may even haunt you like spirits in a haunted house. No matter what you do, those questions won't go away.

Let's look a bit at this new way of thinking. It is more reflective. You develop a new ability to stand back and look at what's going on. You wonder about other people's motivations and feelings. You wonder about your own thoughts and feelings. The little kids don't do that very much.

In the process of your wandering and wondering you can find some disturbing things. You may slowly discover that the way your family does things is not the only way. Going away to college is a real crash course in wandering and wondering.[3]

You may get a roommate your very first semester who believes the exact opposite of nearly everything you learned as a kid. And when you argue, the roommate is not at all bashful about defending her way of looking at things.

You were taught a strict sexual morality, but your roommate sleeps around and doesn't worry about AIDS or going to hell. You were taught never to lie, but your new boyfriend lies like a rug and doesn't apologize when you catch him. You've never been inside a church in your life and you draw a Jesus freak for a suitemate. When you were a little kid, you handled people who saw things differently from you quite simply. You said they were nuts! Anyone who wasn't a good guy like you, was a bad guy. Bad guys were bad guys, that's all. You wrote them off, because you had only two categories for all living creatures: us and them. "Us" are good; "them" are bad.

Oh for the days when things were so simple. Now it's not so easy. You *know* your roommate is a good person, but she's a devout Muslim from some little country in Asia you never heard of. "Oh shit," you say to yourself, "life's too complicated." One way of solving it all for a while is to dump the Malaysian roommate and find somebody from your hometown in Ohio to room with, preferably somebody who agrees with you in everything. You can just try to stay away from anyone different from you. You can build yourself a little cocoon in your sorority or frat house and hope that nobody ever gets inside different from you. I grant you, you can do that. To a certain extent everybody *does* do that.[4]

You'd go crazy if you didn't have some of the comfort of your own folks. I think that's one good reason why Black students socialize with Black students, Whites with Whites, jocks with jocks, Jews with Jews. All of us have a right to spend some time with our own. Pretending that everyone who is not one of your own is some sort of undesirable, is a different thing. Systematically fixing your life so that nobody ever challenges your beliefs is a different thing too. Sticking only with people like you is the mark of a child. My childhood is over and so is yours.

We have grown into an ability to take new thoughts and the beliefs of other people seriously. To be adults we have to use that ability. So the years of youth are years in which a person can experiment to find out what fits. You have outgrown your childhood's mind; you've left the body of a child behind too. The new one you have is larger and more beautiful; it makes demands on you that the old one never did. There are all sorts of new choices to be made because of it.[5] How strange to be taller than your mother or stronger than your dad. That new body certainly underlines the fact that your parents are just people who make mistakes like other people. As you get stronger they are getting older . . . and the position of their authority shifts from the people with all the answers to older advisors whose advice you may or may not follow. They cannot answer the hard questions of career and love that are coming up. You have what they have given you; you have your own childhood years; you have your new friends and your hopes for the future. Out of these you have to fashion a life.

The place of the God whom you may be doubting for the first time in your life? What do you do about those doubts? Who can show you for sure whether or not there is a God? Who can help you see whether such a God is a loving God? Your sharpened awareness will no longer allow easy answers. You know that. Thinking about it and talking about it can help, but my own conviction is that no amount of thinking or reading or talking can give you an open and shut case about God, one way or another.

A very large percentage of you will have to spend some time in a sort of limbo between believing in a supreme being and not believing. I don't think most people can get out of that, not if you spend four years in the presence of so many different kinds of people and so many different systems of ideas in and out of the classroom.

You probably remember from the first pages of this book that I'm not going to serve you up a nice recipe to solve the problem. I will even offer my own doubts that any amount of thinking and reading can solve it. As far as thinking goes, I think you will always wonder as long as you're alive. Put it another way, the odds against God dropping into your college dorm are pretty high. Nobody to my knowledge has ever seen God.[6] The kind of sureness that is like holding something in your hand or seeing with you eyes—you'll never have that.

What does that leave? I need to ask another question.

When you first learned what it was to stand by a friend back in junior high, did you ever know for sure that your friends would stand by you? Even your very best friend? Even your own mother? That lack of absolute sureness probably didn't keep you from making friends and from trusting your mom. There is an element of trust involved here. One of the remnants of your childhood that we haven't talked about until now is trust. Little kids learn to trust their own families. At least one of the most famous people in the field of developmental psychology says that trusting is the very first thing a newborn child must learn and the foundation for all living that perdues throughout human life.[7]

We both know that trust is sometimes betrayed. People you trust the most can hurt you the most. If you managed to survive a divorce in your family, you know that. And yet, could you or I or anyone get through a single week of life without trusting a lot of people? If you didn't trust anyone, you would have no friends. You'd be afraid to leave your room for fear of getting mugged or tricked or somehow manipulated by the untrustworthy people out there. It is human to trust other people; I grant you that trust must be an informed trust. You don't trust everyone the same. There really are some dangerous places and pastimes; you learn not to trust those. The fact remains, you do have to trust some people.

I think that trust is as important in religion[8] as it is in human friendship. And so is honesty. They seem almost to cancel one another out, don't they? As though if a person were really honest, he'd never really trust anyone, knowing that trust always involves taking a risk. Let's leave it there for now, with trust and honesty right next to one another in the search for God and friendship.

I should like to add here, staying with our friendship analogy, that in order to make friends, you must have at least a minimum of leisure. Show me someone who is totally consumed by work, and I'll show you someone with no friends. Making friends takes time; you have to be willing to spend the time if you want to make friends. There's more too. The time you spend has to have some quality. You can't count the time when you are running to class or when you are half asleep or when your mind is elsewhere.

You need to be able to pay attention to really meet someone. You need to listen and respond. You need to be aware of little unspoken messages a person gives out. You really have to be there, all of you. If you do all the talking, you very likely will never get to know the other person. You have to listen and be receptive, and of course you have to be willing to take the risk of liking somebody else, and the risk of caring for someone else. There's a lot to it . . . making friends. And you have to be willing to do all that, knowing that the person you are cultivating may not turn out to be a friend at all.

I think all the points in the paragraph just above apply to the search for God.[9] You have to listen. You have to give quality time to the search. In a way the voice of God, if you can call it that, demands that you be especially at peace and alert.

Maybe it is a fortunate thing that some of the very things you need to keep your own sanity on a college campus are the same things which I think you need to search for God.

There are days when you need some peace and quiet so much that you want to scream, "Shut up!" to the whole world. You have to get out of there and go to a quiet place that fits you. In the other book I have written for college students, *How to Survive in College,*[10] I discussed the need of quiet time for sanity. I suggested that the reader of that book make a list of the places where he or she has found quiet and peace. I think most people have a number of such places.[11] I also think it often happens that they get left behind when you go off to college. Until you find some here, the place can drive you crazy. So make your list of places for yourself and think them over quietly. If you loved the country or an old tree in your back yard, then you have to find something like that here at college. If you had to find a nook that was really quiet for study at home, then look for one here and keep on looking until you find one. Maybe you rode your bike or sat on a bus. In any case the places of the past can be a guide to finding places now.

There are times too, of course. Everyone has times of day and seasons of the year which are especially healing. Are you a late night person or an early morning person? Some people find sunrise an important time. Others feel the same way about sunset. And then there are seasons—Christmas and Easter, spring, fall, and summer. Any of these can be healing time, but you need to notice them.

You need to give yourself permission to give those special times some of your attention. If you love the cherry and apple blossoms of spring, but don't take the time to go see them, you have lost something. If you took early morning walks at home and found the quiet touched you and made you more whole and alive, then don't forget them here.

There are people in your life as well, who are touchstones of what is best in you.[12] People who see what is deepest and best in you. You will need to remember them, to call them back to your mind. Sometimes you will need to write them or telephone. A good long visit is the best of all. Maybe your mother is one of those people, or a childhood friend, or a teacher you had in the seventh grade.

And your prayer? Will it differ from the prayers of your childhood? Of course, because you yourself are different.

Your prayer will be more reflective and inner than your childhood's prayers. There was nothing fake or hypocritical in your rattling off the formulas of your childhood, but to do that now might seem very fake indeed. The deeper meaning is very important now, not just the saying.

You must bring your whole self to prayer, if you are to pray at all. That means your questioning too, your doubts, for the need to be honest remains at the heart of your search. Sweeping your questions under the rug at prayer time is a very basic error. Those questions are not going to stay under the rug; and deep down you have known that. Just as quiet times and places are necessary for good old sanity, so too they are important for prayer.[13] Why?

I think because of the necessity for honesty. It's easy to say prayers when you are coming home two hours late at night or when you think you are pregnant or are afraid you'll flunk an exam. Those prayers are like insurance. You think, "I don't know if there is a God, but it can't hurt to pray that no one will notice my coming in late or that I'm not pregnant." Those prayers are hurried ones during hurried times and they are so wrapped up with trying to get out of something that you might well have avoided, that they can be just an excuse on your part for not bothering to be on time, protected against pregnancy, or ready to take an exam. Such prayers can be seen as childish ways of trying to avoid what you have coming to you. It is quite natural to say them, but they have not enough honesty to be the basis of a good relationship with God. If the only time you are nice to your father is when you are broke and hoping for a ten dollar bill, your relationship with him is very thin. He will know it and so will you.

So, you need some of those best times[14] of quiet and you need to be in one of your quality quiet places. *And* you need something more than just requests. You need to bring to prayer the same things you need to bring to friendship.

Your words need to be *your* words about how *you* feel. You should bring your doubts and your trust, both right together, because both are real. You need to bring that uncluttered mind that you save for your friends, so that you can listen and observe as well as talk. You need not to be hurried, but relaxed and taking your time. When you are with a friend, you don't want to be looking at your watch all the time; that's what you do when you are with someone who is a pest, someone you'd like to get rid of.

So, we have set the scene; we have talked about necessary preliminaries. Can anything else be said? In a certain real sense, nothing more can be said. If you arrange a meeting with a person, you can prepare to be at your best, but you know when it actually comes to conversation beyond the chitchat level, well you just have to wing it. A prepared speech just won't work. Still, there are things you can do to break the ice.

I'm a great believer in talking about the weather. There's nothing wrong with asking another person where his home town is or what his college major might be. Sometimes it helps to offer a small compliment, "I like the way you do your hair," things like that. Sometimes it takes a number of openers or fillers to keep things going. It's perfectly respectable to have a good stock of them; people keep things like that in reserve without even knowing it.

I want to talk with you in the next chapter about the business of "openers" in prayer, but I want you always to know that they are only openers; the real conversation has to just come the way real conversation comes in other friendships. No amount of small talk can substitute for a real conversation; it can help get a real conversation going, but it cannot substitute for it.

Notes

[1] Erik Erikson's biography of the childhood and youth of Martin Luther is a very rich source here. The book centers on Luther's crisis of identity with special emphasis on the religious dimensions of this crisis. Cf. *Young Man Luther* (New York: Norton, 1958), p. 1-288.

[2] Besides Erikson, three authors are useful here. Lawrence Kohlberg has a really penetrating understanding of youth's sense of justice as tied to loyalty for other persons. Cf. *The Philosophy of Moral Development, Vol. I* (New York: Harper and Row, 1981), p. 18, pp. 148-50, p. 410. Robert Kegan is useful here too, *The Evolving Self*, pp. 184-220. As regards a direct treatment of faith and youth, see James Fowler, *Stages of Faith*, pp. 151-173.

[3] My own treatment of college as a place to wander and wonder can be found in *Passages in Teaching* (New York: Philosophical Library, 1982), Chapter One, "The University as Asylum," pp. 13-33.

[4] There is a marvelous description of how a college student learns the complexity of thinking in William G. Perry, Jr.'s *Forms of Intellectual and Ethical Development in the College Years* (New York: Holt, Rinehart, Winston, 1968). I recommend the whole book.

[5] At the risk of boastfulness, I am going to refer the reader who finds Erikson's own work confusing, to two chapters in my own introductory book on Erikson's thinking. Both chapters concern what Erikson calls "the crisis of identity." Cf. *Introducing Erik Erikson* (Lanham: University Press of America, 1987), pp. 39-49, pp. 69-80.

[6] As regards the Hebrew scriptures, I remind the reader that Moses *saw* a burning bush. The Hebrew people were led by a cloud and a pillar of fire

in the desert. Nowhere in the pages of scripture is there a reference to a person seeing God face to face. Cf. Exodus 3/1-ff and Exodus 13/21.

[7]Erik Erikson is the famous man. Check his *Childhood and Society*, p. 247-251. See also my *Introducing Erik Erikson*, pp. 25-27.

[8]Erik Erikson, *Childhood and Society*, p. 250.

[9]Kelly Nemeck has an insightful commentary on Moses' response to the voice coming from the burning bush. Moses said simply, "I am here." Nemeck sees this as a model of simplicity in prayer. Cf. *Contemplation* by Francis Kelly Nemeck and Marie Theresa Coombs (Wilmington: Glazier, 1982), pp. 32-35. For the words of Moses' response, see Exodus 3/4.

[10]Francis L. Gross. *How to Survive in College* (Lanham: University Press of America, 1988) was written before *Searching for God*. Many of its insights are connected with themes I treat here. I refer the reader especially to Chapter Two, "Finding Your Deep Self," pp. 7-15 and Chapter Seven, "God, Buddies, and Mentors," pp. 41-50.

[11]An American witness to the value of quiet places is Henry David Thoreau. I refer the reader primarily to *Walden* (New York: Modern Library, 1937, first published 1854). The whole book concerns the beauty of solitude. I refer especially to two chapters, one entitled, "Sounds," the other, "Solitude," p. 101 ff. and 117 ff.

[12]A fuller treatment of the value of knowing the people of your past appears in *How to Survive in College*, p. 55-61.

[13]I need not remind the reader of the places chosen by the great prophets of Israel for hearing God's voice. Mountain tops and remote places are of special note. Moses went alone to the mountain to receive the law. Exodus 19. He was alone in the desert at Mount Horeb when he received his call. Exodus 3. Jesus, in later times withdrew alone to pray, and told his followers to do the same. Luke 5/16, Luke 6/3, Mark 1/35, Matthew 4/1.

[14]Thoreau has divided *Walden* into a journal-like form, showing what is best in each season of the year for his quiet purposes. He discusses as well different times of day as conducive to quiet. Cf. *Walden*, "Where I Lived and What I Lived For," p. 79-80. See also "Sounds" p. 101 and "Solitude," p. 117.

4

Openers

I want to begin talking about openers with the observation that you have all done this before. I won't be telling you anything new, just putting some old things in a new context.

For want of a better word, I will use the word meditation to describe what I'm talking about . . . and you have all meditated.[1] Who has not sat in his room staring out the window thinking about a friend who is far away? Who has not spent time looking at clouds or a sunset? Who has not dreamed of being a hero or a success? Daydreaming is a form of meditation . . . and you've been doing it all your life. When you daydream you imagine. Sometimes, if you really get into a daydream, you even enter into a conversation with a person you have summoned up in your mind. Meditation is systematic daydreaming. Remember, you can't hurry a daydream; you have to be relaxed and slow. Daydreams, as all forms of meditation, move at a very slow pace.

Accomplished daydreamers can keep it up for as long as a whole class period. Remember daydreaming in class, being lost in another world, so that a large portion of the time went by? Everybody else in the class took notes by the page, except you. Suddenly, at the end of the period, you came back to your normal state of awareness and wondered with a shock where all the time went. Daydreaming is a form of self-hypnosis and so are all forms of meditation. When you daydream, you are aware of something, but in a different way than your normal and more organized form of consciousness.

Meditation is an organized and planned form of daydreaming.[2] Let me give you an example. Suppose it is the beginning of the Christmas holiday and you are on your way home on a Greyhound bus. You close your eyes and recall two or three of your favorite Christmas scenes— perhaps the family gathered around Christmas dinner, hanging up your Christmas stocking as a kid, or the Christmas scene in Bethlehem long ago. These three are your subject matter for your daydream.

Let's say you begin with the first one. You begin by imagining in your mind's eye each person at the table, what the room and the table looked like, how the food looked. You imagine the smells and tastes connected with that dinner—the odor of turkey or goose, the taste of cranberries, your mother's dressing for the turkey, whatever is done in your own family. You listen for the voices; you hear them again, and the clank of the silverware, the laughter, the jokes. You remember how you felt on that day. It is important in daydreaming that you pause when you feel like it to savor the feelings and sights, the smells and the noises. You may even make small words to yourself. You might say to yourself, "Those early Christmases were great . . . how I loved them." You might even want to single out a person there and say hello. "Hi, grandma!" Maybe you just want to linger there letting your mind float, just enjoying the images.

If something completely foreign to your plan comes to your mind, like wondering about your grades for the past semester, you just quietly push it out and go back to your subject. If you have trouble getting into the dream, you might try bringing back the scene one sense at a time. Try listening to the words for a while. To stop and savor an image is a good thing. If you were to spend a whole hour thinking of just a few of the faces of Christmas, that would be a good thing, not a bad one. Finishing all you have planned to think about is not important in this business. People who are adept at meditating go slower than beginners, not faster. Summoning up a scene, remember, is classified as an opener. The important part of the time is what happens once you get going. It is letting your mind flow over these important memories, savoring them. It is small words of wonder or joy or thanksgiving. It is the emotions that come back with the memories. It is the special things you say to yourself when you do remember. A meditation that is also a prayer is merely a matter of subject matter. If you remembered the Christmas scene of the first Christmas—the man, the mother and the divine child—you could go over that the same way you went over a Christmas dinner . . . watching, listening, feeling the cold, gathering the savor of the scene. Here, as before, you linger when you feel like it. If there is some short thing you want to say to yourself, say it. "How cold it was!" or even "Thank you for coming to us." or "Tell me what that first Christmas meant."

I want to remind you that good conversation demands hearing with an open heart. You have to listen a lot in a good conversation. Daydreaming has a lot of listening in it. I myself think that the listening, the drinking in of the scene is more important than what you might feel like quietly saying. Both, of course, are important.

Let me remind you too, that the place where you do your daydreaming is important. Riding in a bus or car is an excellent place for some people. You need a quiet place where nobody will bother you. Your list of quiet places is a good list to consult when you want to bring back something important to you for daydreaming purposes.

The time is important too. You have your list of your favorite quiet times; pick one of those for your daydreaming. They are the result of years of loving; they are tried and true times and places. You have daydreamed in them before, except perhaps you didn't call it that. To let your meditation touch you most deeply, you will be helped to find places and times that occur with regularity in your life. In some people's lives, there is a certain amount of time regularly when they first awaken in the morning. It might be a good idea to take advantage of that time, because it is so often the quietest time of the day. So, there are daily times; they are important. It's as if taking some quiet time is not a luxury but a need for many of us. We need the peace and strength that such times bring . . . and we need it every day.[3]

A parallel to what I am talking about would be study time. As a student you have learned that you learn a lot more if you have a regular time for study during the semester and a good place to do it in. Good grades depend on regular study; there has got to be a sort of easy rhythm to your study life; it must become a part of your day, so that without reminding yourself, you know where to go and what to study at the time you have set aside for study.

Another parallel is eating. We all have eating habits. Some sort of rhythm is a part of everybody's food life. Different people do it different ways, but most people, if they want to stay healthy and enjoy their food, have some kind of dining hours. Good dining demands a certain leisure, as good study goes, and good daydreaming.

It is important to know the difference between study and meditation. Most students know that a person has to study to get good grades. That's pretty clear. What does regular meditation get you? That is often not so clear. A great many people in American society can see the value of good, hard work.[4] Most Americans believe that hard work will bring you success and that success will bring you money. Everybody wants money.

Daydreaming seems the very opposite of hard work. When you are daydreaming you are not working; from a work point of view, daydreaming is a waste of good time. Why do it? Because you need it. It can help you live a deeper life, closer in touch with the values most important to you and the people you care about most. Just as important, quiet time is something everybody needs. Quiet time can help you lead a life that is not just on the surface. It helps you be a deeper person and a more thoughtful person. It allows your most important voices to speak. Those voices are often crowded out in the hurry that characterizes so much of American life, in and out of college.

Really, the best authority for recommending meditation is your own voice. If you are one of those people who has to get away from the noise and confusion from time to time, you'll know what I am talking about. I am talking about a regular way of getting to a quiet place. I want to emphasize that this is just one way. There are lots of others; if you already have a regular way of being quiet, don't abandon it. My suggestions may give you hints for making your quiet time better, but that's all.

If you have experienced the joy of stepping into silence, you will know that there is something good there. I'd like to try to describe that "something" a little bit more. Just what is it? Well, you could call it a very quiet voice which you don't ordinarily hear. A very true voice, but pitched low, so that hurry and worry easily drown it out.

I'm sure that many psychologists would call it the voice of your unconscious. The word "unconscious" does mean unaware. My unconscious (and yours) is a vast area within me of which I am unaware, for the most part. There are times when I get a glimpse of it, but I must be alert and quiet. Much psychotherapy is concerned with putting a person in touch with her unconscious in the hope that its deep understanding will shed light on the hidden sources of emotional upset.

Meditation and quiet are not psychotherapy. For one thing they are not aimed at healing emotional wounds so much as deepening a person's strength and filling out one's understanding of one's self. That deep voice is often the truest voice we have; we need it. People we call deep are always in touch with it one way or another.

Religious meditation goes on the presupposition that down there within you is not only your truest self; it is also the place where you are most likely to encounter God. It's as simple as that. It is helpful to me to think that my own truest voice can speak to me, if I let it. My own desire for honesty and my own fear of being deceived in the whole business of searching for God are important here. I don't want to search for God in the places where I am most easily conned or deceived or manipulated. I've had enough to do with churches and religious con men and women to be very wary of being fooled.

It has been a comfort to search in a place where I am pretty sure the voices are true ones. The people in both Eastern and Western religions who say that God's voice is located most surely deep within us make good sense to me.[5] They are kindred spirits.

I do want to keep this explanation practical, so we might as well tackle some of the practicalities of listening to this voice which is claimed by mystics to be both my own voice and the voice of God as well. Does it speak like a radio? or like another person in conversation with me? I don't think it is usually like a radio at all.

Let's try parallels. Suppose you have a personal problem you want to solve. You wonder whether or not you should break up with your boyfriend. You know that in many ways he's a jerk. He does a lot of things that not only annoy you; he's downright mean sometimes. On the other hand there's something about him that attracts you. He's said some marvelous things; he's a deep person, even if he's so often thoughtless. What a dilemma. You have lots of reasons for wanting to keep him and lots for wanting to get away from him. How to decide? You've tried to figure it out coldly and rationally. That doesn't make the decision easier. If anything, it makes it more confusing. You see so clearly that there are good reasons for staying with him and good reasons for leaving. You've asked the advice of your friends and they are divided. Some are for him and some against. What can you do?

There *is* another way to go. You can follow what your instinct says. One way to do that is to sleep on it. Put it out of your mind for a day or a week. Find something else to do for a while before going back to your decision. Take a trip; go to the movies; stay up all night talking to another friend. Sometimes, after you've given a problem a rest, when you return to it, you will know what to do. How do you know? You just know, that's all. It's not so much that you have found new reasons; it's more like something within you that doesn't give reasons has spoken. For many people this intuitive voice is the truest voice they have in making decisions.

That's the voice I'm talking about. I would hasten to add that it is not prayer's main purpose to find the answer to questions. That is merely one of the purposes. You can take your quiet time as a way of sleeping on a problem, but its uses are far broader than that. Answering questions of what to do or how to do it is only a part.

What are the other parts? The need to rest is one. We really began with that one, for we began with the sometimes horrible stresses of living in college. Meditation is relaxing, but there's more to it; it provides joy and strength. If you bring back your favorite people or your deepest thoughts for review in meditation there is great power there. Bringing things back in a meditative way is not the same as just taking a long sleep. Again, what I'm asking you to do is to remember the joy you have gotten out of watching a sunset or remembering an important person.

A word or two on some practical "how to's" of meditation: stillness is important. Really deep meditation usually requires that you be still yourself. You can sit or lie down, but it is important that your body be still, yet not preparing for sleep. Curling up in bed just the way you do before dropping off to sleep at night is not a good meditation position. Your body knows that certain positions are a prelude to sleep and will act accordingly. I don't mean that you have to sit in the lotus position like a Yogi in India, but I do mean that you should find a good chair and a good alert position that is relaxed. If you do drop off to sleep once in a while, that's not a bad sign. It does mean that you have been relaxed and that is necessary.

Many daydreamers close their eyes during meditation. Some leave them open and fix them on a picture, a scene or any fixed object. When you begin, check your body to see if it is relaxed. A good way to do this is to concentrate on your breathing for a few minutes. Breathe quietly through your nose, feeling the breath going in and out. Then quietly recall your first scene. I do want to underline the basic notion that meditation is not the same as figuring something out. When you meditate you are not planning your day or looking for new reasons for something. It's more like putting yourself in touch with a friend whom you trust and just being with that friend. Do your reasoning some other time.[6]

Once in a while you may experience a time when you just sit there peacefully without any new thoughts or images. That's a good sign. Stay quiet and immobile as long as the feeling lasts. Your meditation times will slowly develop more times like this.

What do you do about all the distractions? They come rushing in from everywhere. Worries, plans, math problems, images of breakfast, you name it. They will always be a part of meditation. I can only tell you that there will be days when you don't have much of anything but distractions. It isn't a good idea to get too upset about them; that only makes them more oppressive and stronger. Just quietly push them out, knowing that they will be back.[7]

I have heard of famous Indian persons of prayer who have learned the art of meditation so well that they no longer had any distractions at all. Frankly, I don't believe it. Distractions are part of the package for most people.

Notes

[1]Look at the opening paragraphs of Thoreau's treatment of "Solitude" in *Walden*, p. 117, his description of sitting in his doorway from sunrise till noon, p. 101. Irene Claremont de Castillejo uses the term "diffuse awareness" to describe a frame of mind very close to what I am talking about here. Cf. *Knowing Woman* (New York: Harper Colophon, 1973), p. 14, ff.

[2]I refer the reader to Ignatius of Loyola's *Spiritual Exercises* for a brief and to the point description of meditation for beginners. Cf. *The Text of the Spiritual Exercises of Saint Ignatius,* (Westminster: Newman Press, 1949. First published in 1548), "Second Week," pp. 36-39.

[3]I refer again to *The Spiritual Exercises of Saint Igantius.* This little book has lasted for 450 years and is still in print. Some of the language is rather warlike and some of the images dated, but it remains an excellent reference for beginners in mediation. Cf. "Annotations," pp. 1-3.

[4]Josef Pieper has written concisely and well concerning the value of leisure and contemplation. He puts special emphasis on just how it is that modern Western people have come to be suspicious of both leisure and contemplation. Cf. *Leisure: The Basis of Culture* (New York: Pantheon Books, 1952), pp. 25-81.

[5]Teresa of Avila, writing more than 400 years ago, spoke of entering deeper and deeper into one's self as a way of getting closer to God. Cf. *The Collected Works of Teresa of Avila, Volume Two,* (Washington: ICS Publications, 1980, translated by Kieran Kavanaugh and Otilio

Rodriguez), p. 283-84. In our own day, Mohandas Gandhi identified his inner voice with truth, and truth with God. Cf. *Gandhi's Truth* by Erik Erikson (New York: Norton, 1969), pp. 230, 397, 412.

[6]I cannot resist quoting Teresa of Avila here. Speaking of intellectuals and prayer, she says, "Although their studies will not cease to benefit them a lot before and after, here during these periods . . . there is little need for learning in my opinion." Cf. *Collected Works of Teresa of Avila, Vol. One,* translated by Kieran Kavanaugh and Otilio Rodriguez (Washington: ICS Publications, 1976), p. 105.

[7]Eknath Easwaran, speaking out of a South Indian Hindu tradition, makes this point well when he says, "I recommend that you do not fight distractions in meditation." Cf. *Meditation, an Eight-Point Program* (Petaluma: Nilgiri Press, 1978), p. 125.

5

The Tradition of Your Childhood

We have talked about identity as being forged out of the remnants of your childhood and the anticipations of the adult years to come. It would seem, at least, that the moral and religious traditions of your childhood would be at least part of the stuff from which you forge a religious identity. There are many societies in which the matter of religious choice would never come up. If you were born in a small village in India, for example, you would be born into a Hindu, Muslim, or Sikh household and you would never question that heritage unless you moved away. I am sure there are some corners of our own country like that, and I am not knocking that kind of life.

It is possible to barricade yourself in your own tradition even here at a university.[1] We've discussed that in an earlier chapter. In order to do so, however, you have to surround yourself with people as much like yourself as possible as well as maintaining a closed mind in class. It can be done; you can do it. I personally don't think you can maintain such a closed door attitude forever without knowing down deep what it is you are doing. We are back to the question of honesty. Honesty is concerned with not hiding from the world around you; it is concerned with not living in a make- believe world. The real world of the mainstream of industrialized countries like our own is a pluralistic world.

When I say pluralistic, I mean that in our world there are many different conventions, many different belief systems, many different religions. Our own Constitution reflects this pluralism when it guarantees freedom of religion, freedom of speech, freedom of the press. To pretend that there is only a single convention, religious or moral, would be like being an ostrich hiding its head in the sand. The idea of that maneuver is simple: if you don't look around, you can imagine that the world is nice and simple, the way you want it. There are simple societies, but ours is not one of them.

At any rate, you *do* come from a family unit of some kind or other. Your family organized its life around a set of values which you learned as a kid. If you didn't have a God and church you had something else as your highest good—maybe the human race, maybe money, but something. What about those childhood remnants? At this stage in your life it is up to you to make a choice. There's no question that what you learned as a child has affected you deeply. You only have one childhood; you didn't choose it; you just got it. You didn't choose your mother or dad or your younger sister or whether they went to the synagogue or stayed home. That was a given and it became part of you.[2]

How about now? Are you just stuck with being Jewish or Catholic or Baptist? Well, you are certainly stuck with having been raised one. Whatever the values of your family were and are, they will have marked you deeply. Where is the choice? The choice lies not so much in what you have been given as in what you can do with it. I can set aside some things in my tradition and keep others. I don't think anyone can just get up in the morning during her first year of college and say, "I'm starting entirely over." You will always carry your past with you. I don't think I can change resembling my mother or walking and talking like my dad. I could change some of what they gave me, but I could not just erase it, like erasing a chalkboard. Furthermore, I wouldn't want to change it all, even if I could. Much of what my family stood for I'm very proud of; it's a part of me. I bet you have some of the same feelings about your family. If you tried to change yourself totally, there wouldn't be much left.

There are some formal convictions, clearly, that you can take or leave. You can believe in God or not; you can go to church or not. This is especially true in a pluralistic society like ours, where such independence is protected by law and prized by the people. Nobody can put you in jail if you decide to quit being a Presbyterian. Your family may get mad at you, but your basic rights as a free person are protected by the government.

What are the advantages of your home training? Clearly, it is what you know best. You'd be a fool to throw it away for no good reason. There are some things in my background that I have learned to be ashamed of; some of those things I learned at my mother's knee. I grew up a racist, for example. Both my mother and dad thought white people were smarter than black people—and I had to reject that when I was older. There's no question that my father thought that he was more intelligent than my mother, because he was a man and she was a woman. He was wrong on both counts, but it took me a long time to see it. The church of my childhood taught us all that we Roman Catholics had the best religion, indeed that we were the one, true faith. Even as a kid I had some trouble with that, because my mother wasn't a Catholic.

At any rate, it took a lot of sweat on my part to come to the conclusion that there were other churches and traditions just as good as my own. I didn't learn that as a child . . . and just because I didn't, it has been a hard lesson to learn. What made it easier was the open society that we Americans live in.

So, you have a tradition just the way I have. It is your task during these identity years to look at it again. To decide how much of it to make more deeply your own, and which parts of it are not worth your allegiance. I think it is a healthy thing to do a little exploring.

You could call it trying on other hats. Trying on new religious hats has many forms. Certainly arguing with your new friends is one form. Experimenting with new places of worship or skipping public worship altogether. Just finding out that you don't get struck by a lightning bolt when you do some experimenting is worthwhile by itself. What a weird experience to discover that your family only knows what you tell them about your experiments! My guess is that as you continue to experiment you will find out more good in what you learned as a child than you thought you would. Whichever of your childhood values you buy into will be forever different, however, because for the first time you were not just handed them on a platter; you chose or rejected them yourself.

As you are going about this laborious process, let me ask you a couple of questions. What do you think about religious truth? Who has it? How strange it is that throughout much of human history religious groups have thought of themselves as God's Chosen People. I don't mean that being chosen is strange. The strange part is thinking that *only* YOUR people were chosen. I certainly felt that growing up as a Catholic. We didn't say that outsiders went to hell, but we certainly thought of other Christians as second class citizens and that other religions were pretty much out of it—Jews, Muslims, Hindus, Buddhists. We called them pagans and were convinced that it was up to us to straighten them out. The best way to straighten them out was to get them to be Catholics, like us.

It has interested me in later years to discover that Catholics were not the only people like this. I found out that other Christian groups frequently figured that *THEY* were the ones with all the marbles. I discovered non-Christian groups such as Hindus and Muslims were sometimes as nearly contemptuous of Christians as we were of them.[3] Frequently, they have fought among themselves the same way different kinds of Christians fought and fight among themselves. What's to be learned? One of the things to be learned is that they can't all be right in their exclusive claims to be the Chosen Ones. Another thing to be learned is how nasty religious people get over their claims. Who wants to join a group of bigots? I can still remember thinking that the odds were mighty long against being born into the one, true, faith. Out of billions of people I happened to land in the only group that had the whole truth? Catholics are a mighty small percentage of the world population. That gave me pause, even as a kid.

There's another side to it too. When you go exploring you'll often find that there is an unspoken assumption in different religious groups that each REALLY has the truth. That makes open conversation hard. Without anybody coming out and saying it in so many words, you know that many committed churchgoers have their minds made up. They are the good guys and everybody else is low life or at least lesser life. It seems common sense to me, and I offer it to you, that there is no reason whatever why a number of religious groups can't be merely good groups.

Your task and mine as searchers gets a lot easier if we are looking for a *good* tradition rather than the best one. It's like looking for a good man or a good woman. God help you if you expect the person you hope to marry to be the best one in the world. What you want is a good person; you'll be lucky if you get a good one. There's another advantage. If you know the person you love is merely good, you won't pass out if you discover she has some faults. Good people all have faults; one doesn't expect them not to. False expectations have ruined many a marriage, just as they have ruined many a religious choice. If you choose a church because it is a good one, a place where you can feel at home, then you won't be surprised that the organization has some kinks in it.

Merely good churches sometimes have ignorant or hypocritical ministers. They always have a sizable number of parishioners who talk about each other behind one another's backs. There are always some who act pious, are regular attenders and contributors . . . who also are unfaithful to their wives, look down on people of other races, cheat on their income tax and are nasty to their kids. "Always" is a strong word; I'm not backing down from it. A good church is a church that has a lot of good people in it, some good ministers of God, and a tradition of fairness and love. That's a lot. What a find you have made if you find a good church. What a fool you are if you leave it because you think some of the people in it are hypocrites.

I dearly hope that neither you nor I expect to find the whole truth in any church. I have learned the hard way that every church, including my own, has taught some very bad things somewhere along the line. Most American churches have taught racism at one time or another. Most have taught that wars were good things for their patriotic parishioners to fight in. Many have taught that the whole of morality is pretty much confined to family and friends—the larger issues of business honesty, a living wage, and peace among nations don't get talked about much in most churches. To be at odds with your church over some of its teachings is not the sign of a traitor; it is a sign of religious maturity. Frequently, being at odds with your church is a sign that you love it enough to disagree with some of its teachings.

Perhaps these issues of good vs. best and truth vs. untruth are best summarized by simply saying that it is a temptation to confuse one's church with God. I expect God to be perfect, to be the best, and to be true. I expect my church to be human, prone to error, and often sinful.[4] I don't worship my church; I worship my God. So, I expect good people in my church; I expect to hear a lot of truth there; I expect to be at home there, but I don't expect it to have all the truth and I would be crazy to expect to find that all the members are good.

As a result of expecting my church to be only good and only to have a handle on some of the truth, my search to find a good one will be easier. If I do settle on one, I can admire the others. I can even say that maybe some of the others are better than mine. I can be a Catholic and have a high regard for Jews. I can be a Baptist and respect Episcopalians. I can be a Christian and believe God will be able to save Muslims, Hindus, Buddhists as well as my own people. I can believe that there can be inspired and inspiring sacred books other than the sacred books of my own people.

How this can expand my horizons! With the attitude I describe above, I can think that Gandhi was a saint, because of his Hindu roots and not in spite of them. I can put Martin Luther King, Jr. on a pedestal as a great holy man of my time, because of his Baptist roots and not in spite of them. If Gandhi was not a good father to his children, I can understand that, because I know he was just a man.[5] If Martin Luther King, Jr. was unfaithful to his wife, I can understand that, because he's just a man too.[6]

I can deplore the stand of my own church on birth control without leaving it. If there are scandals among TV preachers, I don't have to take that as a sign that all Assembly of God churches are corrupt or that their people worship the dollar bill. I can admire the directness of charismatic Christians even if I am not one of them. In short I can live with other religious folk and admire them without demanding that they be carbon copies of my own church or my own faith and without demanding that they be anything more than human. I hope that I can continue to live with myself when I know that I don't live up to the high call of my faith, because I am only human too.

So, I suggest that you take a hard look at your own tradition as you shop around. You may find that it is a good one; you may find a home in your quest where you least expected it, in the tradition of your childhood.

Notes

[1]William G. Perry, Jr. discusses such barricades among college students in what he calls "alternatives to growth." Cf. *Forms of Intellectual and Ethical Development in the College Years,* pp. 177-200.

[2]One of the givens in all developmental psychologies is that every year of life which is completed continues to affect us. This is especially true of the years of childhood. That is why Erik Erikson describes the crisis of identity as a time when "each youth must forge for himself some central perspective, some working unity, *out of the effective remnants of his childhood* and the hopes of anticipated adulthood." *Young Man Luther*, p. 14 (emphasis mine).

[3]The humorous description of a young Indian boy coming in contact with English "barbarians" on a ship bound for England illustrates well an Indian contempt for Western culture. *Punjabi Century* by Prakash Tandon (Berkeley: U. of California Press, 1961), pp. 203-206.

[4]The story of David in the book of Samuel makes my point. David, who was the greatest of the Hebrew kings and priests, was an adulterer, a murderer, and a liar. 2 Samuel 11 and 12. It should be no surprise that the leader of Jesus' apostles was a braggart and at least an occasional coward. Matthew 26/31-75.

[5]Erik Erikson, *Gandhi's Truth,* p. 320.

[6]David J. Garrow, *Bearing the Cross: Martin Luther King, Jr. and the Southern Leadership Conference* (New York: William Morrow, 1986), pp. 313, 361-364, 372-377.

6

Variant Forms of Prayer

Speaking of looking at different traditions, there are many traditions of prayer. The differences in traditions are more pronounced for beginners than they are for people who have become adept at prayer. All prayer seeks union with God. The beginnings of how you get there vary a lot. I'm going to present you with a few variations on what I called "openers" in Chapter Four, for the simple reason that beginnings are important. It is important to get off to a good start, if that's what you are looking for. That start needs to be something that fits you. Often what fits you is in some way related to the tradition of your childhood. It doesn't hurt to have a couple of ways to go, either. Some "methods" are suitable to certain kinds of situations. Let me explain.

Many religious traditions of both East and West make use of the regular recitation of short formulas. The Lord's Prayer is such a formula, as is the Shema of the Hebrew Bible. I want to describe how such formulations can be used as mantrams. The word "mantram" comes from Sanskrit and the use of Indian mystics.[1] The Indian holy man Maharishi Mahesh Yogi has popularized the use of the mantram in the United States in what is called Transcendental Meditation, or simply TM.

I might remind you that most Westerners have used mantram-like short formulas since childhood. Little children use chants the world over when they play. "Ring around the Rosy" is one you probably played as a child. Your night prayers probably took on the aspect of a little formula—something like, "God bless Mommy and Daddy and Uncle Jim and all my friends in Jesus name. Amen." Maybe you said, "Now I lay me down to sleep, I pray the Lord my soul to keep, if I should die before

I wake . . ." There are lots of them. The point about formulas like this is that they become part of us by frequent repetition. When we get older we are aghast that we said them with such little attention to meaning when we were kids. The practice seems downright superstitious. Psychologists tell us that such forms go very deep; those childhood recitations are often not the surface things they seem. Often, they are expressions of trust, trust which is at the very heart of all prayer.

"Now I lay me down" and the "God bless" formulas certainly are in that category. The familiarity and brevity of these childhood formulas make them short expressions of a whole spectrum of religious feelings. They are, as it were, touchstones for a kind of commitment that goes very deep.

Admittedly, we outgrow them as we said them as children. But they live on in adult forms of prayer. Eastern Christians repeat a formula called the Jesus Prayer: "Jesus, Son of God, have mercy on me." Roman Catholics repeat a formula called the Hail Mary over and over while moving the beads of a necklace called the rosary through their fingers. What is the purpose of this seemingly monotonous repetition? There are various answers, but it seems to me that the idea of such repetitions has to do with emptying the mind of the worries and cares that so often run like a theme song through our minds all day long. It is possible to carry a lot of junk around all day in the back of your mind, a kind of perduring anxiety that takes now one form, now another. Today you worry all day about your boyfriend. Tomorrow you worry about a math exam. The next day you spend a lot of time wondering whether you have your eye liner on right. Do you look foolish in the clothes you picked out for today? Will the girl next to you say something in class that will give you a chance to start up a conversation? You can get a beautiful mosaic of junk running through your mind from dawn to dark. Should I do it this way or that way? Did I mess up? Why am I so dumb?

An awful lot of that perduring worry is absolutely useless. It doesn't lead to meaningful change; it just deprives you of peace of mind. Enter the mantram, your handy formula. It is a tie-in with a basic sense of trusting and loving. By quietly repeating it as you drive down the road or walk to class you can empty your mind and heart of a lot of self-defeating worry and fill it with something deep and beautiful. The repetition of the formula itself is comforting, like being held by a friend or being rocked like a baby in a cradle. I think many people who stroll about with a Walkman are listening to music they know and love which has very much the same kind of effect as the use of a mantram.

I should like to add that your choice of formula is important. Take a formula that goes back to what is most meaningful to you in the religion of your childhood. If you grew up saying the rosary, you may rediscover it. Check in your memory the short formulas of your childhood prayer and pick one of them. Try repeating it in times of stress as well as driving and walking times. It may become a part of your life. All traditions of repeating formulas do have one thing in common. That one thing is letting the formula do the work. Don't recite it with the idea of squeezing as much meaning as you can from each repetition. Better just to recite it quietly in a relaxed and unhurried way. The meaning will take care of itself. You don't want to push it.

Another alternate form of prayer consists in taking some prayer you know by heart and saying to yourself short phrases of it, pausing after each phrase to ponder the meaning of the phrase.[2] The idea is not so much to dig up some novel prayer that you never heard of before, but to take an oldie from your background and ponder over it phrase by phrase. The pondering part is the key. It's not so much trying to figure out exactly what the formula means, although it includes that, it's more seeing the wonder and depth of an old prayer which you might never have said seriously before. Let's see if I can give you an example. Suppose I sit in my room or outside on a hill. Suppose I lie in my bed in the morning and say: " 'Our Father,' I wonder what that means . . . calling on God as dad. You could call God something far scarier than father. I always hope my dad will take care of me, that he'll be there for me when I need him. Maybe that's what it means to call God that. I think of being a little kid and holding my dad's hand. Is it supposed to be like that with God? God, I don't know you very well. Sometimes, I think I don't know you at all, but I'd like to think of you as a father. I really would. . . ."

It might be that you could use just the word "father" to use up whatever time you had available, without ever going on to any of the rest of the prayer. If it did work like that, you will have been making good prayer. There is no hurry in this kind of prayer any more than there should be hurry in the use of a mantram or in the meditation form described in chapter four. In this kind of prayer, you move on when you feel you have used up a particular phrase. Then you go on to the next one in the same way. You might be surprised at the riches you discover in some of those old formulas. You don't need a prayerbook or a book of scriptures. All you need is a little quiet time and a place where you won't be bothered.

Listening.[3] This form is even simpler than the last one. Find a place where people won't bother you and just listen to the sounds that come your way. Such a thing can work equally well sitting under a tree in the woods or on a bench in a shopping mall. It can be a very meditative exercise to hear snatches of conversations, the click of heels, the cries of kids, shutting out the sights, you just listen and let your mind wander, listening to the voices of the world, letting them sink in. Not hurrying, you may hear some music or a plane going overhead.

I like to listen while walking in the country; you'd think it would be quiet as you walk along alone down a roadside or through a meadow or on a forest path. There are all sorts of noises if you listen for them. The different calls of birds, the groaning of trees in the wind. You can hear the sound of far off traffic on a road. Rivers and streams make all kinds of subtle noises. I like to walk on stormy days and listen to the thunder and wind and the sound of hard rain. Those are all beautiful sounds. In order to hear and enjoy them you have only to be quiet yourself. You have only to listen.

I might add that I don't think it is a good idea to try to drag pious thoughts into my listening. That's forced and can be counterproductive. Just go with the sounds. If some thoughts come, that's fine. But it's fine if you don't have any organized thoughts at all. You just listen.

A long time ago, I learned to hate taking walks alone, because I figured that walking was a waste of valuable time if I didn't learn something on each walk. So I would be trying to figure out various personal problems in my life as I walked or I would try to remember a lot of different kinds of trees or figure I had to observe just how the people were dressing. That kind of forced activity would be enough to make anybody hate to walk alone. The idea is to be receptive, to wait for whatever comes along. In this case, to listen. Only that. I was a long time learning to be simple on my walks.

Watching. Watching is very much like listening. The rules are pretty much the same, except of course the knowledge that there are a lot of things you can see which don't make any noise.

I recall one time I was making a retreat as a part of my training as a young Jesuit. Our retreat director had given us a lot of heavy things to think about. I'm not so sure it was the things themselves; it was more like there were so MANY of them. My head was full of ideas about what I should do to be a better person, filled with all the things I had NOT done the past year to measure up to being a good student for the priesthood. There were missed opportunities on my mind, all kinds of things I should have done and all kinds of things I knew I should do in the coming year. It was all getting me down. My head hurt; there was nobody to talk to. I was fed up with the whole business.

I found myself walking down to the dock where we kept some old rowboats on a slough which wound its way down to the Mississippi River. I got into one of the boats and rowed for all I was worth downstream, around an island and found myself in the quiet water on the other side of the island exhausted and in a strange place—woods on both sides, no civilization in sight. It was hot there in the sun in the middle of that brown water. So I put on my life preserver, hooked the chain attached to the front of the boat around one of my feet and jumped into the water. It was cool there. I didn't swim, just floated along held up by my life preserver, the boat beside me. I found myself looking at the woods and sky, too tired to think about anything at all. There was a heron fishing at the waters edge. A fish jumped once in a while. I saw a muskrat swim right in front of me on his way over to his nest. I just drifted slowly along, watching, feeling the cool water, letting myself go. Time went by, an hour, two hours, three hours. I could tell by the sun that it was getting late. There was a talk to go to at 5:00 p.m., so I reluctantly climbed back into the boat and rowed home, feeling strangely refreshed. Every instant of time I had for the rest of that weeklong retreat I headed for the river and floated next to my boat. I didn't bother trying to figure out my mistakes of the past year or worrying about the year to come. I didn't think I was praying at all. I just watched the trees, the sky, a few birds, and a muskrat or two.

When the retreat came to an end, I was refreshed and ready for the next year and I think I had spent the first really prayerful days of my life there in the water. It came to me then with a start that prayer has very little to do with trying to figure things out. It has a lot to do with being quiet and letting the spirit work. What I have written to you on the subject of watching all goes back to that experience in the river when I was not much older than most of you.

So, in order to give you a few alternate ways to my main presentation on prayer, these four: the mantram and mantramlike prayers, working through an old formula phrase by phrase, listening, and watching. The alternate forms sometimes fit special circumstances. You can use the mantram well when you are walking or riding. You can work on old formulas when there has been no time to prepare a more formal meditation. Listening and watching go well with places you have found attractive. It is good to have more than one string to your bow, especially when you are a beginner at adult prayer. In later years, as your meditative life grows, it will become simpler. Different methods will become less important, though you will always want to go back to them once in a while. They become like old gloves, familiar, broken in, ready to be used whenever you want them.

In all of them, the key is going slow. Even dozing off for a bit is a good sign. G-o S-l-o-w!

Notes

[1]For an introduction to the use of the mantram, see *Meditation: An Eight-Point Program* by Eknath Easwaran, pp. 57-86.

[2]Ignatius Loyola's *Spiritual Exercises* describe this method with the author's usual brevity and acuteness. Cf. *The Spiritual Exercises,* "Second Method of Prayer," p. 80-81.

[3]It was King Solomon who asked God for a "listening heart." 1 Kings 3/9. A fine commentary on this phrase is contained in Nemeck and Coombs, *Contemplation,* pp. 40- 43.

[4]Watching is a theme of the psalms. The psaims reflect the extraordinary ability of the Hebrew people to see the presence of God in nature, in the workings of history, in day to day life. Here is a sampling of psalms to illustrate what I mean: psalms 77, 86, 106, 107, 145.

Watching is a theme of the gospels as well. You will remember the story of the birds of the air and the lilies of the field; there is a sense of wonder there. See Matthew 5/25-34. The story of the alertness of the virgins is another tale of watching. See Matthew 25/1-12. My own favorite gospel example of watching is the story of the man born blind, the blind man who can see more than those gifted with sight. See John 9/1-41.

7

The Notion of God

I have a feeling we need to get back to the issue of honesty. I want you to know I haven't forgotten it. I want to say again, in the whole business of meditation and God there is a peculiar unity, as though the writer or speaker needs to say everything at once in order to make sense. Issues of God's existence are always part of prayer. You can't separate them out when you meditate. But for purposes of writing, you have to separate them out in the interest of clarity. I want you to know that I am at least aware that you may be impatient; the main issue for you may occur late in my presentation. I don't mind that, if you can stand it, because I don't think the parts of this book make sense unless you have read the whole thing. I ask your patience.

In the interest of honesty, I think it is well to say that all of us, when seeking to listen to or address God, cut her (or him or it) down to meet our own size. All the other persons we know have bodies and are human beings like us. To listen to or talk to the author of all creation puts us in a bind right away. We inevitably address God in some sort of human terms and describe God somehow as more limited than God is.[1] Some of our necessary anthropomorphisms are more useful than others.

I want to give you a list of common ways of seeing God and then to comment on whether they are good ways or not.[2] You can go to God on the general premise that you are dealing with someone who sells oranges. You pick the orange you want; you expect the divine orange merchant to let you have it if you come across with the money. Tit for tat. You pays your money and you gets your choice.

You can imagine God as a slightly crooked politician. If you butter him up from time to time, he'll do you a favor when you need it. Nothing like treating the boss right. Someone who is not sympathetic to this approach would call what you are doing bribery.

You could imagine God as a police officer. The officer's job is to make sure people obey the law. If they don't obey, the cop will try to catch them and see to it that offenders are punished. A good police officer will not take a bribe; she will be fair in enforcing the law. If you mess up, she will do her best to see you caught and punished.

You could see God as an artist. Artists are creative persons. The best artists have great imagination and skill in making all sorts of scenes. Story tellers are artists. Land and seascape painters are artists. Sculptors are artists; they invent people and shapes of all kinds. Artists frequently invent scenes that have never been seen before. Sometimes they invent entire new worlds with colors and shapes that are unique, unlike anything else.

You could imagine God as a play director. Play directors skillfully manage the actors under their direction without depriving the actors of their own individual dignity or skill. Directors manage whole groups of actors all together in concert to bring about a unified narrative in which each of the parts fits in with each other part. The play in which the actors each take part is a larger reality than the individual actors; it proceeds in an orderly manner to a unified and satisfactory ending under the direction of the director.

Being a director is a very complicated task to do well, because each part in the play and each actor playing a part must be respected and yet managed at the same time. And of course the playwright must be respected, the plot and development of the play adhered to and interpreted.

You could imagine God as a lover. A person who is crazy about someone else. A person who is loyal to another beyond all mere justice and fairness. A lover sticks to the beloved through thick and thin, in joy and sorrow. Lovers want to caress and kiss and hold one another. Lovers delight in the company of one another. Love is passionate and forgiving. Lovers don't want to be apart; they long for each other when separated. They cannot get enough of each other. You could look at God that way.

You could look at God as a mother. Mothers are generous givers. They continue to believe in their children when everyone else has given up. Mothers have carried their children in their wombs; they have given birth to them in pain and sorrow. They have known them from infancy. They have fed and clothed them; they have listened to first words and later sorrows and dreams. Mothers are the first and last lovers of their children. Mothers love deformed children, dishonest children, willful children. Mothers love their adult children too—successful and unsuccessful.

You could look upon God as a father. A father's love begins with birth, later than a mother's; it is less successfully described than a mother's love, but it is very like it. A father's love has to do with presence to his children. Whatever his other work, he will be present to them. Often it is not so much what he says that counts to his children; it is what he is. Good fathers are like old lions.

Now, there's a list for you. All these images of God are terribly limited and limiting, but they are all very commonly used for God. How you speak or listen to God very likely has a lot to do with your image of her—or him—or it. For the present, I am going to leave you with those images without further comment. To keep the images coming, I would like you to see some images of God suggested by our own times. I want to do this in keeping with the idea that any notion of God will transcend whatever it is to be human. The most evocative notions of God will need to be put into images which especially are at the heart of modern learning.

As a developmental psychologist I am aware that there is something peculiarly modern about an image of the universe, the world, the creatures of the world, including human beings as being part of a developmental process. Before Darwin, most people thought of the world and the creatures in it as unchanging.

Today we study the development of individual humans in developmental psychology. We study the development of animal forms in evolutionary theory. We study the development of the universe in various forms of development through astronomy. What sort of God does a developing universe have? We are looking at a universe on the move, possessed of a mysterious thrust toward complication, development, wholeness. Almost as though the whole universe were alive.[3]

If older world views saw much of the world as fixed and static, we today are inevitably drawn by our natural science into seeing everything as growing. Any notion of a Divine Creator would involve a creator who is active in the universe, for we no longer see creation as an act of God which was done once for all, but an ongoing process which has perhaps just begun. The image of a God who created the world and then left it is ill-suited to an understanding of today's world. If there is a God at all, it seems most sensible to me to see reflections of that God in the billions of years of change in the universe, in the tens of millions of years of change of the planet earth, and in the millions of years which measure the development of homo sapiens.

A great part of the wonder and marvel of our universe is taken up with seeing it grow and change. An image of God at odds with this strikes me as blasphemous. Yet some religious thinkers in our own day want to keep such an image away from God in order to protect bygone religious traditions. Talk about straining out a gnat and swallowing a camel!

I would like to suggest that the reader make use of the marvels of contemporary developmental science in thinking of the godhead. God as identified in part with the process of development itself.

Two ways suggest themselves as further fruitful uses of this image. I can look at the marvelous beauty of the growing world outside me or I can look at the equally marvelous world at the center of my own consciousness. I am reminded of a passage from a contemporary novel, Alice Walker's *The Color Purple*.[4] A woman named Shug Avery is explaining her notion of God to another woman, her friend Celie. I want you to see how active a God Shug describes, how involved in the universe . . . speaking in the context of sexual love, Shug says:

> Oh . . . . God love all them feelings. That's some of the best stuff God did; and when you know God loves 'em you enjoys 'em a lot more. You can just relax, go with everything that's going, and praise God by liking what you like.
>
> God don't think it dirty? I ast.
>
> Naw, she say. God made it. Listen, God love everything you love—and a mess of stuff you don't. But more than anything else, God love admiration.
>
> You saying God vain? I ast.
>
> Naw, she say. Not vain, just wanting to share a good thing. I think it pisses God off if you walk by the color purple in a field somewhere and don't notice it.
>
> What do it do when it pissed off? I ast.
>
> Oh, it make something else. People think pleasing God is all God care about. But any fool living in the world can see it always trying to please us back.
>
> Yeah, she say. It always making little surprises and springing them on us when us least expect.

Behind the simple language of the rural South is a very active God, present in its world, author of the world's continually changing beauty. Earlier of this passage, Celie asks Shug what God looks like. Shrug replies,

> Don't look like nothing, she say. It ain't a picture show. It ain't something you can look at apart from anything else, including yourself. I believe God is everything, say Shug. Everything that is or ever was or ever will be. And when you can feel that, and be happy to feel that, you found It.

I think looking right into the heart of the world we live in, walking, as Alice Walker says, "in a field of purple" and noticing it is a very good way to discover both the world and God. I agree with Walker when she has Shug say, "It ain't something you can look at apart from anything else, including yourself."

Learning to look at the world is really what this book is about. God, as Shug says, "Ain't something you can look at apart from anything else, including yourself." I like quoting that line twice. Maybe you'll notice it, if I do that!

In this case, the emphasis is on the world outside a person, signified by "the color purple." Shug underlines "admiration" as something God likes. I would add, and I think it is understood in these passages, that admiration of the world around you is a way to know God. Maybe you can see now why the two chapters you have already read on forms of prayer put so much emphasis on seeing, feeling, and listening. Walker's word, "admiration" sums them up. It's a question of paying attention to what's already there. That might be a historical event, like the birth of Jesus or the Exodus. It might be something right in front of you right now. In any case we are talking about being very much present to the world and savoring that presence.

The poet says:

> The world is charged with the grandeur of God. It will flame out,
>   like shining from shook foil;
>   It gathers to a greatness, like the ooze of oil
> Crushed.[5]

There are many poets of God's grandeur. Most of them talk of the world around us as echoes of God. A few of them look inward for those echoes.

Teresa of Avila thought that the prime place for finding God was within herself.[6] She speaks of the journey to God as going farther and farther within ourself, as though there were seven houses within each of us. As we turn farther and farther inward we get closer to God. For each house is within each other house, the last one being the farthest in and the closest to God.

I think that most Americans are familiar with the general notion of God's presence in the world, even if we are such a hell bent for leather people that we don't often take time to admire the world's various "fields of purple." I would remind the reader that Alice Walker refers us not only to the outer world but to the inner one as well, when she says, "God ain't something you can look at apart from anything else, *including yourself*." As an extrovert people, we Americans are more at home, most of us, with the outer world. The inner one is much more likely to be a scary place which we prefer to keep at arm's length.[7] How much easier it is to go to the family doctor for a broken leg or a case of measles than it is to go to a counselor or psychologist for something troubling us within.

What do you suppose Teresa of Avila meant by those seven houses within us? It is true that most religions worthy of the name are concerned with a person's spirit. There's more to religion than outward observance of rules. There is concern with an inner quality, "Blessed are the clean of heart, for they shall see God."[8]

You yourself have felt a revulsion for people who put on an outward show of correct behavior without bothering with inner attitudes, like honesty, kindness, or courage. We call such people "hypocrites" or "fakes" because they pretend to be one thing, while in actuality they are something else. Your spirit has a lot to do with whether or not you are a good person. Teresa surely meant that. One thing she did not mean in her discussions of the inner life was an equation of goodness with intelligence. She didn't think that smart people were closer to God. Being intelligent is only peripherally related to the inward journey she talks about.[9] I think she *did* mean the quality of being a deep person, a person who is not all on the surface. People talk of depth that way in ordinary conversation, but what do they mean? It's not easy to describe. Deep people are not flighty; they mean what they say. They consider what they are doing; they will go off and think about it. They are in touch with themselves. Who wouldn't want to be a deep person? It sounds nice, but how do you do it?

I am convinced, and so was Teresa of Avila, that part of it has to do with spending some time alone on a regular basis.[10] If you are busy all the time, if you have a lot of noise in your life day in and day out, it is very hard to hear your own deepest and truest voice. I'm sure that was a part of why Thoreau went off to the woods to spend two years living alone in a small cabin he built himself.[11]

Thoreau's dramatic experiment may sound weird to you, but his aim was quite practical. He wanted to be able to hear his own voice and the voice of the world around him, lest he become lost in the babel of voices and other noise that was a part of living and working in town. I don't think you have to move to the woods for two years to do this. Let's see if I can explain.

When I was sixteen years old, my family went to California for the summer. There were family members who lived on a ranch just east of San Diego. I had an aunt there who let all the teen-agers in the family stay with her at her ranch for the summer; we were supposed to work taking care of orange trees and the vegetable garden in return for our lodgings, but we spent an awful lot of time riding, hunting, swimming and singing around the piano. There were about ten of us. That ranch was a lot different from any place I had ever been—the orange trees, the hot dry nights, the singing, all my newly discovered cousins. We were all together day in and day out for six weeks. For me it was like magic. I never had so much fun; I never laughed so hard. It was hard for me to believe that it was really me. Those cousins accepted me. They kidded me about being crazy about one of the girls who was my age, and they were absolutely right. It seemed that every day we did something magic—we swam in the surf at La Jolla, we rode horseback in the hot nights under the moon, we went sailing in the San Diego harbor, we went quail hunting very early in the morning when the light was fresh and magical and everything was very still.

It was as if I found a new self that summer; one I didn't know—a funny self, a self that could make up games and jokes and songs, a self that was strangely attractive to my bewitching cousin Jane . . . and this was me! I don't recall ever having had so much fun or attention just dumped on top of me before. I blossomed like an Easter lily. I got over being shy and timid and self-conscious about being skinny, but I never did get over my amazement that the others thought I was somebody special. It amazes me to this day.

That summer was different from living in the woods like Thoreau, but it was a summer filled with amazement and wonder—partly at the beauty of Southern California, partly at the charm of my cousins, but most of all that they clearly thought I was somebody special. Jane and I were the mascots of the group, the talk of the town. Me! It was a summer of wonders. I think was in "a field of purple" all day long for six weeks. A marvelous place, but my biggest wonder was that I was at the center of it and people marveled at me. That summer did not last forever, just a few short weeks, but I have not forgotten it. It has remained with me as a sort of touchstone of joy and beauty. I carry a light inside of me that began there. That light is still glowing. I know there is beauty in the world and I know there is beauty in myself and nobody can ever take that away from me.

And where is God in all this? Not apart from it, but in it. Not like a character in a movie or play. God was no Obiwan Kenobi, no Yoda, no special person, some sort of celestial E.T. I think that God was in it *all*, not apart from it . . . like yeast in bread dough, like oregano in spaghetti sauce, like the chocolate flavor and color in chocolate ice cream.

That's what Alice Walker's character Shug means when she says that God "don't look like nothing. It ain't a picture show. It ain't something you look at apart from anything else, including yourself."

Special places, special times in your life and in mine bring a certain experience of wonder. The poet e.e. cummings expresses this:

> i thank You God for most this amazing
> day: for the leaping greenly spirits of trees
> and a blue true dream of sky; and for everything
> which is natural which is infinite which is yes.
>
> (i who have died am alive again today,
> and this is the sun's birthday; this is the birth
> day of life and of love and wings: and of the gay
> great happening illimitably earth)

> how should tasting touching hearing seeing
> breathing any—lifted from the no
> of all nothing—human merely being
> doubt unimaginable You?
>
> (now the ears of my ears awake and
> now the eyes of my eyes are opened)[12]

So much for the ecstasy of seeing, hearing, touching, tasting both the outside world and the world within. So much for the "highs" of prayer. You may recognize them; you may not. One thing both you and I know is that old homely truth, "You can't be high all the time." Maybe you've tried; then you know for sure that for every high there's a low, and that most of the time is just plain ordinary. I want to talk to you about prayer and the nitty gritty of ordinary times. The highs are very important, but they never last.

When I was a grade school kid, I had a group of older cousins that used to come through my home town of St. Louis on their way east to college. They always stayed a few days with us going and coming to school. They were from New Mexico and could play Spanish music on guitars. When they were at the house, the whole place was filled with the sound of Mexican music, with St. Louis cousins (especially if they were girls), with long legs and deep voices. I remember them all as having huge feet. They were godlike figures to me. And most of them were polite but distant to the little people of the house, of whom I was one. One of them was different. He used to come out to the kitchen and read the comics of the evening paper to us. He told us stories with a deep Spanish accent about Red Ryder and Uncle Gordo. Just made them up out of his head. Looking back on it, I think he loved us as much as we loved him . . . and anytime he and his friends came to town, he always found time to spend with us in the kitchen or back yard for stories and jokes. When he went off to war, he sent me a real bazooka shell and a Japanese battle flag with holes in it which I never doubted were real bullet holes. After the war, when I myself was a college student and he was in graduate school, he came down to see me, driving his new, green

Mercury convertible. I thought I was having a visit from one of the gods. Of all my older cousins, I remember him the best. My sisters and I worshipped the ground he walked on.

What a surprise for me to find that my godlike older cousin told my mother that his own religious faith had sort of dried up and lost its feeling. I remember getting up my nerve and asking him about it, hoping that he would tell me this wasn't true. That was not the case. He told me at some length that he had long dry periods when everything in his native faith lost all its feeling. That was the first time I remember hearing someone whom I KNEW was a good person talk about hard times or at least unfeeling times in his religious life.

Years later I reads the famous Spanish mystic, John of the Cross. He described ordinary adult prayer as characterized by what he called the dark night of the soul,[13] as if it was the lot of everyone sooner or later to be in a faith condition marked by darkness instead of light. This darkness was such that one could not see much with the eyes of faith, a kind of condition of spiritual blindness. I think it was what my favorite cousin described as dryness. I have learned since that it is the lot of most people.

Maybe a comparison will help. I have a whole bagful of vivid memories of being in love, going right back to grade school. The summer I described to you earlier in this chapter was a summer of being in love with my cousin Jane. After a good many loves and a good many years, I asked one of those loves if she would marry me. She agreed and we tied the knot. I remember very well one particular evening in my office at St. Louis University when we sat in chairs facing each other for a very long time saying little, just looking at each other. We began in the late afternoon, just sitting there. The shadows in my office gradually lengthened; it became dusk, then night, finally the moon rose. And all that time we just sat there, looking into each other's eyes. Time seemed to stand still; its passing only noted by the gradual oncoming shadows of evening, then night, then the soft light of the moon. That was a special evening. I will never forget it. Today, almost twenty years later, it is different between us. The early raptures are gone; we do have some special times still, but they are not the same as the early ones. We are more used to each other, like a pair of hands that have touched one another off and on for years. You might call us a pair of old shoes; we are broken in. We have been through a lot together. We have fought and struggled and loved. We have lived our every day lives together; we share two sons; we have learned not only to play together; we have learned to work together and that all is not lost if we have a tiff, or even a real fight.

What's the difference between the early love and what came later? The later love is deeper; it has survived a lot of ups and downs, and it is usually much quieter; it is usually less emotional. It is certainly better informed; I didn't know her faults in those early days and she didn't know mine. It isn't all skyrockets and flashes now. More ordinary. But deeper, steadier, I'm sure of that, even if it is harder to see, surrounded as it is in the ordinary business of home life.

The language of old friends is the language of everyday. There is a darkness there; the bright light of new friendship and new loves is faded, the sureness is gone. But the sureness of new love is often cocksureness. Life's later shadows require more trust. Later love is deeper. I would suggest to you that in the language of old friends there is a rich area for searching out God. I would suggest to you that if you have had a time or two of passionate religious conversion, that conversion is like young love. If Teresa is right about God's inhabiting the deepest places in the heart, then the experience of old love is a good place to look, because old love is deeper. God is more present there, if I may talk that way, than in the hot joy of passion. I think you have to have an old friend or two to know what I mean. I don't want to dwell too much on old friends, because at your age most of your friends are new, and you must of course search the experience that you know now. In later years the verses of the poet W.H. Auden, written in his mature years, will resonate in your heart as they do in mine:

> . . .but when I try to imagine a faultless love
>   Or the life to come, what I hear is the murmur
> Of underground streams, what I see is a limestone
>   landscape.[14]

Young or old, however, you *do* and will have ordinary times and days. If you seek times and places of quiet, the still, small voice[15] will be there for you to hear. It has this advantage over the great songs of high times; it is deeper; it is more frequently there; it is more reliable.

We have talked of searching in great times and ordinary times. What about bad times? Can they be good times to search? I think so.

A number of years ago I had a neighbor who was at that time the head of the counseling center in the university where I teach. I remember once asking him what kind of people are the ones counselors and psychologists can help the most.

He grinned and allowed as how a counselor could help almost any kind of person who had really hit bottom.

"Frank," he said, "when they walk into the counseling center with blood on their noses, we can help them."

You get blood on your nose if you have fallen flat on your face. You know you are in trouble; you march into the counseling center, maybe you stagger in. You go where the secretary sends you. Your first words are, "Doc, what do I do?" You are ready to work, because you are desperate. Times of desperation are often times of receptivity. You might be open to look anywhere or try anything if all your old tricks for avoiding trouble have failed you.

How well I recall going to see a chiropractor for the first time. My family has physicians in it; most medical doctors think chiropractors are crazy. I had learned that lesson well. "Stay away from chiropractors," said all the wise people of my childhood. What I didn't know was that chiropractors are very much aware that M.D.s are against them. You don't see the chiropractor unless you are desperate! My back had been sore for two years; I could hardly walk. I had seen my family doctor and several specialists. They all shook their heads, clucked, and gave me pills to relax my muscles. "You have to expect this," they said in chorus. "You are just getting older." The chiropractor was my last chance.

The first time I saw him, he cocked his head, smiled and said, "You've tried everything else, haven't you."

He helped me a lot, but I never would have gone to see him if I hadn't been desperate. Victor Frankl, a psychiatrist who was interned by the Nazis in World War II, spent a lot of time watching his fellow prisoners in the concentration camp where he was held. They all knew that sooner or later each one would be herded into the camp gas chamber for execution. It was just a matter of time, unless they were rescued. How strange that these desperate people frequently found new meaning in the few days or weeks that most of them had left.[16] One would have guessed that most of them would have despaired when they realized that they were marked for execution and that until that day came, they would systematically be starved, forced to work in the freezing cold without proper clothing, forced to live in such crowded conditions that they were like human sardines packed into a can.

Frankl noticed that many of them found new depth to their lives. He concluded that the desperate times had something to do with many prisoners finding meaning in the short span of life remaining to them. It was as if they were able to see things they never saw before. They noticed human dignity they had missed before; they often learned a new compassion for their fellow prisoners. Some of the most selfish discovered a kind of generosity within themselves that they had never before experienced. Some of them saw for the first time in their lives a divine dimension they had never before seen or felt.

If we return to Alice Walker's novel, a central theme to the whole book is the triumph of the Black woman, her survival against the odds.[17] Trouble is at the heart of her strength and vision. Listen to Shug, speaking to her friend Celie:

> Here's the thing, say Shug. The thing I believe. God is inside
> you and inside everybody else. You come into the world with
> God. But only them that search for it inside find it. And some-

times it manifest itself even if you're not looking, or don't know what to look for. *Trouble do it for most folks, I think. Sorrow, lord, feelin like shit.*

Strong words, those, pointing to desperate times, "feelin' like shit" as a key to deeper meaning, in this case driving a person deep within herself to find God.

I feel an echo in Shug's words from the mysterious Servant of the Hebrew Bible. Isaiah the prophet describes a man who has suffered, linking that man to liberation of the Hebrew people. Somehow sorrow is connected with freedom and liberation:

> He has no form or comeliness; and when we see Him, there is no beauty that we should desire Him. He is despised and rejected by men, a man of sorrows and acquainted with grief. And we hid, as it were, our faces from Him; He was despised, and we did not esteem Him. Surely He has borne our griefs and carried our sorrows; yet we esteemed Him stricken, smitten by God, and afflicted. But He was wounded for our transgressions, was bruised for our iniquities; the chastisement for our peace was upon Him, and by His stripes we are healed. All we like sheep have gone astray; we have turned, every one, to his own way; and the Lord has laid on Him the iniquity of us all.[18]

Not only in the lives of people in fiction, the people of the desperation of death camps, and the great figures of the Bible can suffering bring depth.[19] I mention these examples because I am sure that in your time in college most of you will have some desperate times. Most of you will experience days, weeks, even months when your world seems to cave in, when you will feel rejected and perhaps even despised. There will be times when you too will be "feelin like shit." College is too new and strange a world for you to escape hard times.

You too may well get to the point when you will try almost anything to get relief. There is a good chance that you will find within yourself some deep strength, some new vision that you never would have found if your days were smoother. I do not mean by this to say that you should avoid getting help from the counseling center or wherever else you can get it. I *do* mean to say that all the counseling centers in the world can not get you out of hard times in college. There is a chance in those desperate times to grow, to become a deeper person. There is a chance that in those experiences you will experience the presence of God and that this experience will help you.

We both know that I cannot experience your life for you. I'm not the one who can listen and look for you. You have to do that for yourself. I can tell you a little about my own times of listening, of seeking and finding, but I cannot do it for you. I hope that my experience and the examples I have quoted for you will make it possible for you to be a better searcher.

At this point I'm suggesting to you that you return to the images of God detailed in the beginning of this chapter: the orange merchant, the police officer, the artist, play director, lover, mother and father. After thinking about it you may find one or other of these images more useful than the others. You may find that some of these images were useful and made sense to you when you were a child but not now. You may find that some of these images are ones you have kept from your childhood right up to this moment without having given it much thought. Some of childhood's images are fine in childhood but destructive in a more mature world. Some of these images need to be left behind if you are to stand on your own two feet. Which ones? I ask you to think about it. I know very well that it is your choice, not mine. I know too that you may have some images, both good and bad, that are not on that list. Think about those too. There are inner and outer images, modern and ancient ones, images of passion and exaltation, everyday images, images of sorrow. If any one of them speaks to you, I have done my job as helper. Good hunting.

Notes

[1]Thomas Aquinas refers to God as "being itself" or "subsistent being," and labors mightily to escape the limitations of human figures in attempting to describe the divinity. See *The Basic Writings of St. Thomas Aquinas, Vol. I,* edited by Anton C. Pegis (New York: Random House, 1945; original in Latin c. 1260 A.D.) p. 131.

[2]James Fowler is quite explicit in showing the images of God common among people at different ages and stages of development. I don't want to summarize his findings here, because I want you to decide for yourself which images you find meaningful. If you want to check up later, then look in the Index to *Stages of Faith,* "God," p. 327.

[3]Pierre Teilhard de Chardin has written extensively about God in a world understood as evolving. His best non-technical book on the subject is quite short; its style is poetic. See *The Divine Milieu* (New York: Harper and Row, 1968).

[4]*The Color Purple* is a novel very rich in its comments on God and the paths people take to God. I have reproduced one of the richest chapters in Appendix A of this book. See Alice Walker, *The Color Purple* (New York: Harcourt, Brace, Jovanovich, 1982), p. 164-168.

[5]This poem is reproduced in its entirety in Appendix B of this book. Its author, Gerard Manley Hopkins, has written many poems with similar themes to this one. See *Poems and Prose of Gerard Manley Hopkins,* selected by W.H. Gardner (Baltimore: Penguin Books, 1953).

Other poets concerned with reflections of God in the world are e.e. cummings, Charles Peguy, T.S. Eliot and Lawrence Ferlinghetti.

[6]I have mentioned Teresa in Chapter Four of this book. The name of her work on the seven houses within the soul is *The Interior Castle*, in *Collected Works, Vol. Two*, pp. 263-452.

[7]C.G. Jung speaks of "the primitive fear of and aversion to everything that borders on the unconscious." Cf. *The Basic Writings of C.G. Jung* (New York: Modern Library, 1959), p. 481 ff.

[8]Matthew 5/8.

[9]See chapter four of this book, footnote 6.

[10]It is amazing to me, and perhaps to the reader that Teresa recommends two hours a day of quiet time for her sisters. Modern commentators, writing for people seeking quiet while remaining part of the hustle and bustle of the world advise less time daily, but are insistent on regularity nonetheless. See *Meditation* by Eknath Easwaran, p. 42 ff.

[11]The "Conclusion" of *Walden* has a most eloquent passage on the adventures of discovering one's inner self. See *Walden*, pp. 285-287.

[12]This poem is reproduced in its entirety in Appendix C. I would recommend e.e. cummings, as a poet of wondering and marveling. *100 Selected Poems* by e.e. cummings offers a large selection of these. Make your list of favorites, (New York: Grove Press, 1926).

[13]John of the Cross, "The Dark Night," in *The Collected Works of St. John of the Cross* translated by Kieran Kavanaugh and Otilio Rodriguez (Washington: ICS Publications, 1979), p. 323.

[14]W.H. Auden, "In Praise of Limestone" from *Selected Poetry of W.H. Auden* (New York: Modern Library, 1959) pp. 114-117. T.S. Eliot speaks eloquently of dryness and darkness—and of solitude. See *Selected Poems* (London: Faber and Faber, 1954). I recommend his "Ash Wednesday," p. 81-89. Charles Peguy is a more accessible poet than either Eliot or Auden, and he writes beautifully of dryness, night, solitude, and hope. See "Sleep" and "Freedom" in *Basic Verities* translated by Anne and Julian Greene (Chicago: Logos Books, 1943), p. 129-143. See also his "Hope" and "Night" in *God Speaks* translated by Julian Green (New York: Pantheon: 1945). Gerard Manley Hopkins, already quoted in this book, has a series of sonnets and other poems with the common theme of dryness and abandonment. See *Poems and Prose of Gerard Manley Hopkins* selected by W.H. Gardner, pp. 60-68.

[15]The prophet Elijah heard the voice of God "in a still, small voice." This is a famous text in the book of Kings. It is often used to show how God's promptings to the human heart are generally not spectacular or noisy, 2 Kings 19/11-13.

[16]Viktor Frankl, *Man's Search for Meaning* (New York: Pocket Books, 1959), p. 56-58, pp. 178-183.

[17]Triumph through suffering is a frequent theme in the novels and poetry of American Blacks. Alice Walker is but one voice among many. I refer the reader to the poems and autobiographical works of Maya Angelou, to the novels of Toni Morrison and Margaret Walker. Of special note is *I Know Why the Caged Bird Sings* by Maya Angelou (New York: Bantam, 1969).

[18]This passage is from Isaiah 53/2-6. There are four passages in Isaiah about a chosen servant of God. They are called the Songs of the Servant. Here are the references to Isaiah: 42/1-7, 49/1-6, 50/4-9, 52/13 to 53/12.

[19]It is surely superfluous for me to mention in this context the four accounts of the passion, death, and resurrection of Jesus, narrated at the end of each of the four gospels.

8

Why Go to Church?

Why indeed? It would seem that there are a great many reasons for not going to church. If you have discovered the value of silence and solitude, why join the crowd? If you are aware of the fact that there are church goers who pretend to be pious on the outside but within are spiteful, why be in the company of such hypocrites? If you realize clearly the need of being honest with yourself in religious matters and you are honestly uncomfortable within the walls of your church, why go? To begin with, I do heartily agree with the notion that one ought to question church attendance. If you never question it, you will never be an adult. Period. Kids go to church or stay at home because that's what the family does. When you are older, you *can* go the kid route if you want to, but it is harder because you do have a new sharpened awareness. It's hard to pretend that you don't.

If you are in your late teens or in your twenties, you are in the process of deciding what you stand for. You are taking a second look at all sorts of things. This whole book is written with the premise that the crisis of identity includes within it a crisis of religion. So far, we have talked about God and prayer in this context. Church falls under the same principles. You need to look again; you will probably have to experiment to find out where you are. When you experiment, you change your behavior. You try new things and new thoughts.

How can you experiment with church attendance? You can try not going. You can try going. You can go to synagogues, churches or places of prayer that you've not tried before. And of course, you can talk about it. Experimenting with church is regarded by some people as a sort of betrayal. As if you must stick with the practice of your childhood no matter what. People who think like this almost always have decided for themselves already what the best way is. Frequently they have forgotten that they themselves did some wandering around before they arrived at a solution. Usually such people want you to act the way they act. Usually they want you to go to church where they go to church or to stay at home the way they stay at home. They have a vested interest in a certain way and they want everybody else to do it their way.

One of the reasons we have freedom of worship guaranteed in our constitution is to prevent people like this from forcing others to be carbon copies of themselves.[1] The reason for separation of church and state in the United States is to guarantee that religious enthusiasts will not have the power to coerce other people to copy their churchgoing or staying-at-home. Nobody can make you go to church or stay at home in this country. The presumption is that adults can and should make up their own minds once their childhood years are completed. Not only is it good psychology to make up your own mind, your freedom to do so is protected by law. So, experimentation of some kind is in order.

That means that church attendance cannot be defended any other way than seeing if it makes sense. It must stand on its own feet.

Well, why then? I think the basic reason for any church attendance has got to be some kind of sharing what the people who attend have. I like this quote from Alice Walker:

> . . . . Celie, tell the truth, have you ever found God in church? I never did. I just found a bunch of folks hoping for him to show. Any God I ever felt in church I brought in with me. And I think all the other folks did too. They come to church to *share* God, not to find God.

A church is God's house because real live people bring that God into it. If they don't, God isn't there. Why share a good thing? Good question.

You could ask, "Why go to a party?" That's a good question too. It brings up surely the fact that not everyone is a party goer. Some people are very private with their joy. I don't think that means they are selfish.

You are only selfish if you refuse to share what you have, but there are a lot of different ways of sharing. There are a lot of different kinds of parties and celebrations just as there are a lot of different kinds of churches and places of worship.[2] Quaker services have very long periods of silence in them when no one speaks at all. Some Baptist churches have a tradition of people shouting back at the minister as he speaks. In other churches people show their emotions freely; they dance, speak in tongues, and even roll on the floor. There is an incredible variety of music in churches and synagogues including places where there is no music at all.

What should you be looking for? An opportunity to share what you have and a place where you can be comfortable sharing it. I should add to the idea of a place that there are usually people in the place. So, people you can be comfortable with too.

I've never heard of a church in which all the people were good. Maybe there is one somewhere, but if I were you, I wouldn't hold my breath until I found one. Church people are just plain people. They are good sometimes and bad sometimes. Some are mostly good and some are mostly bad. If you expect the body of people going to a given church to be all good, that's too bad, because it isn't like that. We have discussed this issue in the context of taking a second look at the tradition of your childhood, but it bears repeating here.[3]

What do you look for in a congregation? I think you should look for people who are compatible with you. I think you should look for good people too, inspiring people, people who lift you up and give you courage. Such people, we both know this, also gossip about others, are sometimes mean, sometimes two-faced, sometimes selfish. If a church required its people to be perfect, neither you nor I would be allowed in. You will remember that the greatest of all the kings of Israel had a lot of faults. He was vengeful; he was an adulterer and sometimes stuck on himself. But he was also a great poet and musician; he was loyal to his friends, courageous in battle, and capable of admitting his faults. His name was David. By the same token, one of the great apostles of Jesus was a braggart and a loud mouth, not to mention being just plain stupid and narrow of vision. His name was Peter.[4] Well then, I suggest you look for a *good* congregation, not a perfect one. That way you won't have to pretend that you are something other than what you are if you want to join.

It is important to see that you yourself see a church as a place where you can share and give to the others. In good churches you give as well as get.

Maybe the question remains, "Why have any church at all? Why can't I do my sharing at work and at home? There are plenty of situations where I am in groups without my having to find or invent another one." I agree. A church has to offer something special or it has no reason to be. You and I both know fine people who are unchurched. There's no escaping that.

It gets down to this. A great many people need other people of like mind to help them hang on to what is most precious to them. The sole purpose of places of worship is to help people nourish the God dimension in their lives. There are different kinds of churches because there are different kinds of people. You look for a church that has your kind of people in it.

When you go there, you celebrate what you believe in the same way you celebrate your birthday on a certain day, the birth of your country on a certain day, or a birthday of a person important to your country, like George Washington, Abraham Lincoln or Martin Luther King. The purpose of churches is too keep alive your religious beliefs and to help other people keep theirs alive. Jews celebrate the fact that they are Jews in many ways; one of those ways is at temple. The ceremonies they have in home and temple remind them who they are and what they stand for. Jews celebrate Passover to keep in mind the great first deliverance from slavery they experienced under God's leadership long ago.[5] They remember Moses and Aaron and Miriam and the other great heroes of their people. Those stories and celebrations remind them that they must live up to their heroes of the past and that their God today is the same loving God who rescued them from Egypt long ago.

Christians remember the events of Christ's life in church. They remember the early followers of Jesus—Mary of Magdala, Peter, Paul and the others. They are reminded that the death and resurrection of Jesus brought freedom to the early Christians and that the early church is still alive today.[6] That the Father of Jesus is our father still.

Church is meant to underline and nourish the bond between church goers and their common belief in God. If it doesn't do that, it's not doing its job. It will never do that unless the people bring their God into the church, as Alice Walker has noted. Good churches do this; bad ones don't. I believe that there are many good churches as well as some bad ones.

I for one think that it is foolish to imagine that one church is the true one. All the churches struggle to be true to God; none of them succeed completely. I do not look for "the" one, true church.[7] I look for a church where I am at home, a church that tries hard to be true to its tradition, a church where I can be helped to nourish my beliefs and be of help to others. I do not confuse my church, which is human and struggling, with my God. I hope I never worship my church or expect it to be perfect, because that is idolatry. My church is a place and a people who help me worship God.

Notes

[1]Here is a great chance for me to quote those few lines from the United States Constitution that have so much to do with our freedom to make religious choices in the U.S. I quote here the first amendment to the constitution. *"Congress shall make no law regarding the establishment of religion, or prohibiting the free exercise thereof;* or abridging the freedom of speech, or the press; or the right of people peaceably to assemble, and to petition the government for a redress of grievances" (emphasis mine).

[2]Professor Harvey Cox underlines the vital function of celebrating what you believe in *The Feast of Fools* (New York: Harper Perrennial Library, 1969), p. 6-30.

[3]See Chapter Five of this book, "The Tradition of Your Childhood."

[4]See Chapter Five of this book, footnote 33.

[5]Exodus 3/3-16.

[6]Luke 22/19-22.

[7]I am reminded here of the book of Jonah, which points so clearly to the holiness of other peoples besides the Hebrews. I think as well of the great priestly prayer of Jesus in John's gospel, where Jesus prays for unity among those who will come after him. What a commentary this is on the bitterness and rivalry between different Christian bodies! John 16/20-22.

9

Prayer and Morality

This is a hard chapter to write, because the whole issue of morality is very wide. College students are often wary in discussing it. Nobody wants to say what is right or wrong for anybody else.

Still, the period of life in which most of you find yourselves is one in which you are stuck with deciding what you stand for and what you stand against. Everyone has something left over from childhood, nonetheless, most of you find yourselves presently in a period of life in which it's true. Those "remnants" we have discussed before, but the remnants of your childhood do not include your newfound awareness of other people. Lawrence Kohlberg notes that most people in the crisis of youth, the identity crisis, have recently become aware of one another in a new way.[1] You become aware of other people's inner lives. Little kids don't think much about the intentions of other people.[2] As you gradually begin to see that other people have inner ups and downs, inner strengths and weaknesses, you have a foundation for deeper friendships than those of your childhood. You will remember that we discussed this in the context of prayer in Chapter Three.[3]

You begin to feel for other people as you come to recognize the existence of mental anguish. Compassion and loyalty are beautiful new sentiments. Little kids are much more pragmatic in their relationships. They generally operate on a tit for tat morality. The idea of doing something for someone else just because that person is a friend is foreign to most children. But it is not foreign to your world or to mine. One of the things you and I both stand for is being loyal to our friends. One of the things that makes us mad is a friend telling on another friend. Oftentimes we have a similar kind of loyalty to our families. There is usually

72

a terrible dilemma if our families want us to do one thing and our friends want us to do something else. Being betrayed by a friend or a parent, that's serious business. I don't think I would be far wrong if I said that friendship and loyalty are the keystones of morality for most of you. A good person can be seen as one who is true to her friends. A good mom is a person who is loyal to her kids. A good father will be there when you need him. Bad people are people whose intentions don't fit their appearances, people who are one thing on the inside and something else on the outside.

What has any of that got to do with God or prayer? That's the question of this chapter. We need to review.

Early on in this book I tried to make a connection between getting some quiet time and staying sane in college.[4] Put in a less extreme way, there is a connection between some time apart from noise, and hearing your own deepest and best voice. That is your most reliable voice in your task of finding yourself. "To hear, one must be silent," says the wizard to the young man in one of my favorite novels.[5]

You can go a long way in being a moral person if you are in touch with yourself. I add that in my opinion one of the very best places for seeking God is in your own deepest self. I have not hesitated to call moments of real silence by the name of prayer. How is there a connection between being a deep person and being a moral person?

Perhaps if we turn it around, you'll see it. I think people who live on the surface all the time are thoughtless people. They aren't aware of their own depth and they aren't aware of the inner part of anybody else either. Part of being a good person or a loyal friend is being aware of other people's inner feelings. If you are unaware of the feelings of other people, you will ride roughshod over them; you will hurt other people without knowing it. You will not be a compassionate person or a loyal friend if you live on the surface all the time.

I wish I could say that all people who were deep were good. It's possible to be a very thoughtful person and a bad person as well. Maybe thoughtful and deep doers of evil are the worst people of all, because they can hurt others much more deeply than the thoughtless ones. The great villains of history have been thoughtful people. If you really know what you are doing when you cut somebody up, you do a more thorough job. Can you remember someone you really trusted, whom you felt really understood you? Who really cared for you? Such a person could do you more harm than all the thoughtless snobs in the world. I'm sure you have some of experience of that. You never forget the betrayal by someone you really trusted and thought highly of. It doesn't happen often, but when it does you never forget it.

We may conclude, therefore, that becoming a deeper person, more in touch with your whole self, does not guarantee that you'll be a true friend or a loyal parent. This much *is* true, however: there is no such thing as deep friendship or loyalty for people who live their lives only on the surface. Deep friendship and loyalty come from deep people.

There's a connection to be made, one that words on a piece of paper cannot do justice to. I've mentioned it before; here it is again. Those deep voices are hard ones to hear. But if your ear is well tuned, if you have a listening heart, you will be in touch with them. And so, here I say it, if you are in touch with what is deepest in yourself, you will be in touch with God.

It was King Solomon long ago who asked God for a listening heart, for he knew that in the possession of such a great gift he would be close to God.[6] Put it another way, the deepest thing in any of us is love. There is a famous letter in the New Testament, which says it very clearly: "God is love; and one who abides in love, abides in God, and God in that one."[7]

Indeed, the great summaries of the law in the Jewish Torah put the matter bluntly. "You shall love the Lord your God with all your heart, with all your soul and with all your might." "You shall love your neighbor as yourself." Those two pieces are quoted by Jesus in Matthew's gospel as summarizing the whole law. What I want you to see is that they are right together: love of God and love of your neighbor. I don't think you can separate one from the other and be true to any great religious tradition.

If a more modern quote will help you, let us take the words of a man in *The Color Purple*. He is called simply "Mr.__." He has been a bad man for much of his life. He connects his own change of heart to learning to marvel at the world.

> Anyhow, he say, you know how it is. You ast yourself one question, it lead to fifteen. I start to wonder why us need love. Why us suffer. Why us black. Why us men and women. Where do children really come from. It didn't take long to realize I didn't hardly know nothering. And that if you ast yourself why you black or a man or a woman or a bush it don't mean nothing if you don't ast why you here, period.
>
> So what you think, I ast.
>
> I think us here to wonder, myself. To wonder. To ast. And that in wondering bout the big things and asting bout the big things, you learn about the little ones, almost by accident. But you never know nothing more about the big things than you start out with. The more I wonder, he say, the more I love.
>
> And people start to love you back, I bet, I say.[8]

"The more I wonder, the more I love." That's food for thought. So, we have made a connection between a sense of wonder and seeking out quiet time. We have put a sense of God very close to a sense of wonder. We have connected love as a summation of all morality with that same sense of wonder. You can say all that in a short time, but it takes a lot of living to understand it. Would I go so far as to say that if you seek to have a sense of wonder that everything else will take care of itself? Can a person say, "Seek out times of silence and then do what you want?" Is living a life on the surface the same as being a bad person? I think I would say "Yes" to all of those questions. You can find out for yourself. It's not necessary to take my word for it. All I can do is tell you what I have learned and suggest that you try it. If I have a word of caution, it would be to say that the process of connecting wonder with God and love takes a long time. I think it is the work of a lifetime.

I hope here to anticipate a question. There are a lot of laws that bind us both. There are state laws, federal laws. Every family has unwritten laws and rules. Colleges have laws. Every religious tradition has laws.

How can anybody be so simplistic to say, "Love and do what you will."[9] That seems a bit slick, to put it mildly. Seems as though if this is true, then there really is no point in all the many laws that you and I have to live by or pay the price of breaking them.

I'm not backing off from what I have said, but you are right in wanting an explanation. I think it gets down to this, the old matter of what's inside you. All good law is for the protection of the people. That's why we have speed limits for cars; that's why we have fair packaging laws for groceries; that's why it's against the law to steal, assault somebody, or kill someone.

If you tried to keep the law with nothing inside, your observance of the law would be a joke. Either you really wouldn't keep the law or you'd be doing it just for show. That gets us back to hypocrites. Hypocrites are people who keep the externals of the law, but inside themselves they don't care. They do want to be respectable and to receive the perks of being law abiding citizens. They are more interested in being noticed than they are in being caring.

There has to be something inside to go with external observance to make law effective. What is that something inside? The most basic law of all, the simple law we have already quoted, the law of love. That's what has to be inside. What needs to be underneath speed limit laws? Drivers who genuinely care about other drivers. What needs to be behind a manufacturer's labeling merchandise according to fair packaging laws? Care for the consumer. What needs to be behind observance of laws against stealing, assault, and murder? A reverence for a person's property, a person's body, a person's life.

That's why the Jewish Torah, the law of Christ, and the laws of religions in general can boil down all teachings to one word: love. Caring is what it's all about.[10]

I'd like to add a corollary. If the inner spirit is the backbone of keeping the law, it is also the backbone of decisions of conflict of law. Again, the idea part of conflict in law is not complicated. The law of love is not only the spirit for observance of law, it is a higher law as well. Put simply, people come first. I don't think anyone has to explain to a person working as a domestic in an affluent household that it's all right to make off with a little extra food. Poor people have always known that they have a right to live. What you need to survive you can take from somebody else's surplus, law or no law. Why? Because you have a prior need. Taking care of loving your own always comes first. The law of love makes all possessions relative. I have a right to what is mine only up to a point; it is not an absolute right, for it is conditioned by the higher law of love of my neighbor. Cain's question to God rings down the ages, "Am I my brother's keeper?"[11] The law of love has a simple answer, "Yes." If I am unwilling to admit it, my brothers and sisters in need can take what they can get away with.

Before anyone gets too bent out of shape with such a statement of hierarchy of laws, let me remind the reader that our Constitution in the United States guarantees life, liberty, and the pursuit of happiness to all citizens . . . "one nation under God, with liberty and justice for all." That principle supersedes any lesser ones in American law.

So, we have an order of importance in law informed by an ethic of love. We have a spirit in which to keep laws, both sacred and profane, informed by an ethic of caring. If a person is justified in breaking a legitimate law, that justification lies precisely in a higher law of caring for one's fellow human being. I can only break a law if I am in the process of keeping a more important law. Compassion is at the heart of any good system of laws as well as at the heart of any legitimate breakage of laws, as Gandhi and Martin Luther King have shown so dramatically earlier in this century. Gandhi broke many an English law in India in order to help his fellow Indians gain possession of their own land, but he absolutely forbade vengeance against or hatred for the English oppressor.[12] By the same token Dr. King broke segregation laws between Blacks and Whites in order to gain for Black Americans the same rights guaranteed in our Constitution for all, but he refused to hate his White opponents as well as being willing to take the punishment which breaking unjust laws brought down upon his head.[13]

I suggest to you that a deep interior life was the key to the morality of both Gandhi and MLK, and that it is the key to morality for you and for me.[14] Divorce the inner spirit of love from law and you have a travesty of justice.

Notes

[1]Lawrence Kohlberg, *The Philosophy of Moral Development, Volume One* (New York: Harper and Row, 1981), pp. 148-150. See also Chapter Three of the present work, "Youth's Prayer."

[2]Kohlberg, *ibid.*, pp. 147-8.

[3]See Chapter Three of the present work, "Youth's Prayer."

[4]*Ibid.*

Coretta Scott King reports a conversation with MLK in her kitchen during the Montgomery bus boycott in January of 1956. King had been sitting alone at the kitchen table, despondent, his head cradled in his hands. He reported to her: "At that moment I experienced the presence of the Divine as I had never experienced Him before. It seemed as though I could hear the quiet assurance of an inner voice say, 'Stand up for righteousness; stand up for truth; and God will be at your side forever.'" Coretta Scott King, *My Life with Martin Luther King Jr.* (New York: Holt, Rinehart, Winston, 1969), p. 124.

Ervin Smith, researching the ethics of the late Dr. King, comments on the role of religious experience in the life of the emerging civil rights leader: "As King moved from his graduate studies into the center of the civil rights movement, the philosophical and hypothetical idea of a personal God became subordinate to the personal God of his religious experience who was ever near, ever present, and with whom he was in constant companionship." Ervin Smith, *The Ethics of Martin Luther King, Jr.* (New York: Edwin Mellen Press, 1981), p. 27.

[5]Ursula K. LeGuin, *A Wizard of Earthsea* (New York: Bantam, 1968), p. 18.

[6]See Chapter Six of the present work, "Variant Forms of Prayer," footnote 37.

[7]I John 4/8.

[8]Alice Walker, *The Color Purple*, p. 239.

[9]See "St. Augustine of Hippo," quoted in *A Dictionary of Classical and Foreign Quotations* complied and edited by W. Francis King (London: J. Whitaker and Sons, 1904), p. 70, #547.

[10]See Appendixes D and E.

[11]Genesis 4/9.

[12]Nirmal Kumar Bose, *Selections from Gandhi* (Ahmedabad: Navajivan Publishing House, 1948), p. 225-227.

[13]Martin Luther King, Jr., "Letter from a Birmingham Jail," in *Why We Can't Wait* (New York: Mentor Books, 1963), p. 82-89.

[14]Gandhi says: "The man of prayer will be at peace with himself and with the whole world, the man who goes about the affairs of the world without a prayerful heart will be miserable and will make the world also miserable." *Selections from Gandhi* by N.K. Bose, p. 12, #34.

10

The Problem of Unbelief

Very early in this book, I noted that I was at least aware that the process of searching for God in college is all of a piece. Most aspects of it all happen at the same time. It is hard to write about, knowing that the reader sees a number of different problems all rising up with the one under discussion. One of the problems that is intertwined with the whole business is the matter of belief and unbelief. Let's try it all by itself or if not that, let's give it center stage in this chapter. This is a good place to put it at the center, because we have already talked about prayer and morality and thus have a framework in which to talk belief.

Can you pray and be an agnostic? I'll define an agnostic as a person who has major doubts about God. Under this heading I would put not only doubts about the existence of God. There are other major areas of doubt. Does God care about me? Does God care about us all? Does God really have one chosen people, chosen in preference to all the others? Those are just a few major problems. The purpose of this book is not to provide answers to these problems. Such answers go far beyond the scope of this book, indeed definitive answers go beyond the scope of any book.

The question I want to tackle here is this: Can a person pray with any sincerity while at the same time having major honest doubts? It is my own opinion that a college student who has any depth at all will have all sorts of doubts about God. Show me somebody with no doubts and I'll show you somebody who has never thought about it. In a very real sense, all modern people are agnostics, whether they want to admit it or not. Try getting into a discussion about the existence of God sometime. One of the very first things that will come up is the simple fact that no one has ever seen God. I'm not going to bother quoting Hebrew or Christian scriptures to you. You can look that up for yourself.[1] You can also ask around; you can examine your own religious life too. If you know someone who claims to have seen God, I'll bet you don't trust that person. And you yourself? Be honest; think it over. If you have seen God, you might as well toss this book out right now.

You and I part company right here. If you haven't and have a group of friends who are similarly in the dark, maybe I can help.

When I say that I don't believe anyone has ever seen God, I'm taking the other senses for granted. I mean as well that no one has ever heard God speak or touched God or smelled God or tasted God. Not the way we see each other and hear each other. Not the way we touch each other or smell perfume or like the taste of chocolate ice cream. Again, go to your experience; talk to other people you know.

It's true I associate certain smells with God, like the smell of incense or the smell a beeswax candle gives off. But these are associations rather than anything else. I don't really think God smells of beeswax or incense. I just learned those smells in my church as associated with worship.

By the same token, when some Christians talk about their discussions with God, I don't think they are talking about what you and I mean by normal human discourse.[2] I've not met anybody who claims he can call God on the telephone or who gets letters from God.[3] The discussions people refer to are inner conversations; the voice of God would not come out on a tape recorder. We are talking here of inspirations coming from within. We are talking inner voices and inner pictures. There's the rub. How do you know which inner voices are godly and which come from other sources?

We need examples. What if I wake up in the night with a tremendous desire for a chocolate ice cream cone? What if I wake up scared out of my wits by a bad dream? I can remember a few years ago having a nearly overpowering desire to become a distance runner; I was almost fifty at the time. That same year I had a powerful desire to go back to writing poetry. There was a period in my life when I had a recurrent desire to kill myself. I've had lots of powerful desires to kiss or make love to at least ten different movie stars, not to mention dozens of other attractive women who have come and gone in my life. I've felt the desire to punch someone in the nose so many times I couldn't count them. I've had powerful desires to be a priest and a married man, both.

Well, how am I supposed to know if these "voices" within me come from God? I want to add here that I haven't listed anything here which I considered trifling at the time; all of these voices were insistent ones.

I want furthermore to let you know as a reader that I take my voices seriously; I take your voices seriously too, and I hope you do as well. This part of this chapter is not written to put down inner voices or to take them lightly. What I am trying here to do is to ask both you and me how you and I are to tell if any of these voices are from God. I want to reiterate here something one of Alice Walker's characters said about God.

But what do it look like? I ast.

Don't look like nothing, she say. It ain't a picture show. It ain't something you can look at apart from anything else, including yourself.

This same character in *The Color Purple* says:

The thing I believe. God is inside you and inside everybody else. You come into the world with God. But only them that search for it inside find it.

You've read both those quotes before in this book, but I want you to see them here in the context of seeing and hearing God.

If we say for the moment that God's voice is generally not apart from the voices we all hear and that God's form and shape is generally not apart from the forms and shapes that we see in our everyday lives, then one thing is apparent. We must be very alert to the sounds and shapes and colors of our world to sense God within it. It is not so much a matter of shutting the world out as letting it in. It is as though we must be at our very best—our most intelligent our most receptive, our most alert. I say this because I frequently hear people imply that faith is blind. As though you should park your reason, your intuition, and your senses at the door when you deal with God. As I see it, the very opposite is true.

The question remains, how do I know which of my hunches, intuitions, and visions are from God.

I hope it's not too obvious to say that if I am to find God, I am unlikely to find Her or Him when I am least alert or most gullible.

I have had lots of bad ideas and mistaken hunches. Haven't you? I have had sudden brainstorms that later proved to be ridiculous. Let's try some examples.

I can remember wanting to be a college football player so much that I would have killed to get to be one. I can also remember that I was nearly six feet tall going into the eleventh grade. I weighed a hundred and eighteen pounds, had terrible coordination and was slow on my feet. That year it came clear to me that my long cherished voice which told me I could be a football player in college was not a true voice.

Who has not been deceived by the voice of romance? I have a favorite poem which illustrates how a person can be deceived by an inner voice. See if you get the picture:

See
   it was like this when
            we waltz into this place
   a couple of Papish cats
            is doing an Aztec two-step

And I says
      Dad let's cut
  but then this dame
         comes up behind me see
           and says
        You and me could really exist

> Wow I says
>> Only the next day
>> she has bad teeth
>> and really hates
>>> poetry[4]

Who has not heard that inner voice saying, "Wow," only to discover the next day "that she has bad teeth and really hates poetry." I have, and I'll bet you have too, perhaps not just the same as the poet's "Wow!" but not entirely different either.

I'm going to begin by saying that I am often deceived by my inner voices. They are often all I have to go on in making a decision, however. Very frequently those voices are true.

How do I tell the true inner voice from the false one? Well, duration is important. My own best voices persist. I can't get away from the best ones. The hunches that quickly fade are often not reliable ones. Part of the test of a good voice is its persistence. I mean over a period of days or months or even years.

Another test? That voice must, in the long haul, bring me peace rather than disturbance. Good voices often scare me to death in the beginning. A lot of the time they concern a really difficult challenge, and I'm afraid. If I have the courage to give my voices time, then I will know if, after at first scaring me, they bring me peace. Peace is the sign of a good voice, but it often takes its time coming. Persistent voices that over a period of time bring me peace of mind ought to be listened to.[5]

There's another test. The test of reason. I don't care how much I want something, sometimes my reason makes it very clear that my dream is impossible and that my voice is mistaken. I just couldn't avoid the hard evidence of a skinny, awkward body equipped with very slow legs when it came time to evaluate my desire to be college football player. I also couldn't avoid the fact that I was cut from my high school's B squad in my junior year of high school. My dream had to die; it just didn't stand up to the facts.

I had a student once who had a longstanding desire to be a medical doctor. He wanted to be a doctor in the worst way. There was a problem; he was flunking eleventh grade math and his overall grade point was about 2.5. I was relieved when he changed his dream to wanting to become a professional chef. He didn't need all that math to go to cooking school; a 2.5 grade point was just fine too. His dream of being a doctor just didn't stand up to his abilities. It was the cold, hard facts of reason that brought him to see that his hunch had been a bad one.

Another good test of inner voices is the test of confrontation.[6] Bad voices thrive on remaining partially hidden; they have a way of tantalizing a person by giving the person a glimpse of something that seems beautiful or attractive. One of my sisters was once in love with a really handsome boy. He was tall; he had a beautiful rosy complexion, blue eyes, and a shock of blond hair that set off his long body with just the right amount of carelessness. Amid all his bodily splendor was another tantalizing characteristic; he never talked! Who knows what marvelous things he might have, hidden beneath that veil of silence! The longer my sister trailed him, the more fascinating the silence became. I used to listen in on her conversations with friends on the subject of the silent one, who was also very elusive. He was to be at a certain bar on a Friday evening. My sister made it her business to be there, a place called Culpepper's Lounge, but she only got a glimpse of him as he downed a single beer and vanished out a side entrance never to be seen again that evening by the huntress. Well, after months of stalking him, the moment of truth came rather unexpectedly. Out of this divine man came a squeaky voice asking if she wanted a light for her cigarette . . . . and after that came a very unexciting and interminable discussion of an upcoming football game. Later she told a friend (with me listening in, of course), "I *knew* I should never have talked to him! I just knew it!"

The point of the story is that my sister got plenty of hints that Kobusch, for that was his name, had not an interesting idea in his head, but she just couldn't stand the thought. It was much more fun stalking him, missing him by a hair's breadth, evening after evening. The chase was far more fun than the encounter. She didn't want to know the truth. Kobusch was solid stone between the ears; his voice sounded like a door closing on a Coke bottle; he had all the charm of a young pit bulldog, except when he was silent and seen from a distance. And my sister didn't want to find that out.

Let me try one more time. A few years ago I was having an awful time getting along with one of my sons. I was despondent; nothing seemed to work. The voice of worry was persistent; I could not dislodge it. It followed me around from my cup of tea in the morning until I fell into an exhausted sleep at night. If I woke up in the middle of the night, it was there. Its message: "You are not getting along with Bill; it's your fault . . . and it's going to be like this between the two of you forever. FOREVER!"

One morning I got up with the resolve to pay visit to an old friend, a gifted psychologist, and to talk the whole thing over with him. Even before I actually made the appointment to see my friend, that terrible, sly voice of despair was weakened. As soon as I took steps to do something about a real problem, that terrible feeling of despair left me.   The problem with Bill remained; it is true. I still had to figure out how to make peace with my son. But the terror was lessened. I had stopped running from my enemy; my panic was over. I thought of an old saying, "They can't chase you if you won't run."

Good voices stand up under scrutiny. Bad ones like to skulk in the shadows of your mind. If you decide to look carefully into them, they often go away. I might add that you have to go through with the confrontation process. If I had skipped the appointment with my counselor, my despair would have slipped right back in to my consciousness.

This particular example contains within it an addition to the idea of examining one's voice with cold logic. The idea of another skilled person is the addition. A person you trust can be an immense help in discerning the origins of your voices.

In all the examples I have just named, the effort was to distinguish good intuitions from damaging ones. But I have said nothing of God. Well? I simply do not believe that God has a separate voice for most of us. The voice of God is precisely *in* my own best voices and my own best visions. Alice Walker is right, "It ain't a picture show. It ain't something you can look at apart from anything else, including yourself." ... "only them that search for it inside find it."

I know there is a further question. In finding or seeking to find your own best voice, who gives you the right to identify that voice with the voice of God?

We are very close to the bottom line, it seems to me. I don't have any tricks for this one. I *do* recognize this as a fair question, even a necessary question. It is a question that has been with me all my adult life. It isn't just a part of your life; it is a part of mine too.

Here's what I do with it. Here is what I say.

"God, in my tradition you are presented as a loving God, a God who seeks us out. We are presented as people who ought to be ready to listen, but You are the one who does the talking. I have done all I can to be open to the best voices I know. It is up to you to find me. There's nothing else I can do. I simply won't try to invent a vision or pretend I hear a voice. From the earliest stories in my tradition you have come to my people. Not the other way round. You spoke to Moses and Abraham. You came to them. This is true of all the great people of God in the Jewish scriptures: the great prophets and judges. It is just as true in the Christian scriptures. You took the initiative.

"Now, I have done what I can. It is up to you to find me. What I once thought was my problem, finding you, is much more your problem than mine. I can prepare to be as sane and as much my best self as I can, but you are the one who must find me. At heart I know I don't have to force anything. I will just try to be ready. Now, (damn it!) it's your problem!"[7]

That's how I do it. If I hear a divine voice in the human voices around me and in my inner voices, it is because that dimension was there and somehow made itself heard. I know full well that I will never be able to measure it or to separate it out from other voices. I will do my best to discern my good voices from the ones that seek to destroy me or diminish me. That is all I can do. This is my condition, and as far as I know from talking to friends and acquaintances it is the way it usually is with them too.

In this sense my dealings with God are always in a degree of darkness; they will always be somewhat shadowy. This is how it is. Just because God's voice is always part of all my other voices, does not mean that I am a fool to think it is there. It does mean that I can never prove it's there. It does mean that I need to be open and at my best to hear it most of the time. Sometimes I hear it when I am not open or ready at all, but my best chance of being aware of it is when I am most aware of myself and the world around me.

An important point here is to remember that you and I are both members of a people, the American people, who pride themselves on getting the job done.[8] We are a "can do" people. It is a compliment among us to label a person as someone who can "make it happen." It is a terrible temptation to bring this attitude to the last step of searching for God. It is very possible to think that I am responsible for the finding. It is possible to forget that at the end, after all the preparation, it is God's job to speak and be recognized.

That's not just true with God, of course. If I love someone very much, I can do a lot of things to prepare for her loving me. I can be around; I can be attentive; I can try to be my best. What I cannot do *ever* is to force the words "I love you" from her.[9] She must say those words and she must say them in a way that I can understand. So it is with God. The reason I put so much emphasis here at the bottom line is because I know that a person can cause endless worry to himself thinking that he can "make it happen." That "making it happen" stuff doesn't work in friendship and love and it doesn't work with God either. You do your part, heave a sigh of relief, and know there's nothing more to be done by you.

Suppose now, you are a careful and hardworking seeker of God's voice, and after all this time, nothing happens.

What then?

Your situation reminds me of a story about a man who was a follower of Gandhi. The man knew that Gandhi required his followers to live a very simple life. The man saw the wisdom of this; he didn't want to be distracted from being a loving and non-violent person by all sorts of possessions that might weigh him down and somehow lessen his commitment. But there was a problem; he was a learned man; he loved to read and had a large library in his home. He said, "Gandhi, your counsels about living a simple life make good sense to me, but I have a greedy mind. I just don't want to give up my books."

Gandhi replied simply, "Then don't give them up. As long as you derive inner comfort from anything, you should keep it. You will know when it is time to give the books away. When the right time comes, you will recognize it."

And so I say to you. I think God is very creative. A lot of the time God hides from us. We would like neon lights and big arrows saying, "Here's the place; or This is the voice." We don't get them. Some people never sense the presence of God. Are those people the Bad Guys?[10] I don't think so. Are they less sensitive than those of us who claim that we can discern the presence of God in our human voices and intuitions? I don't think that is true either.

I think there are a lot of ways to skin a cat. I think there are many ways to do almost anything. I think there are many different forms of friendship. A lot of the time my best friends don't seem like friends to me at all, even though all the while they are true to me. Friendship is filled with paradox. Perhaps you have found that you have become closer to your mother or father now that you have left home and gone to college. In the beginning of your college life it may have seemed that you'd never be close to your mother or dad again. Yet later on, it has often happened that sons or daughters feel far closer to parents or loved ones left at home than they ever did before. Sometimes a person has to leave home for a while for a relationship to grow. That's the paradox.

Other times people who have been friends for years and years have a hard time understanding each other and no longer feel close. This is certainly true of married people. It was true of my own mother and dad. Let me explain.

When my mother was seventy-five years old, she contracted a very malignant form of cancer. Shortly after the cancer was discovered, she went off to the hospital. She left my dad after fifty years of married life and she never came back to him. He felt betrayed and angry that she had left him. He never got over it either, even though all of us knew that she was certainly not deserting dad the way he took it. She cared a lot for him all through her final illness, but he didn't feel it.

And suppose you don't feel the presence of God? Does that mean that you are not one of the privileged ones? I don't think so. It certainly is not a call for you to be upset or to try to fake it. It may be that such an absence is a sign of privilege or growth. The absence of God may be a prelude to a deeper relationship, just as your leaving home for college might have been a prelude to a deeper friendship with your mother or dad. I'm not just making this up. The lives of the great mystics in my tradition of Christianity almost always have great, long periods in their maturity when they have no sense of God's presence.[11] It really is like that.

I am not so foolish as to tell you the reason; I don't know. What I do know is that often in our experience of friends whom we can see and touch, there are periods of dryness, lack of feeling, and lack of understanding. My father's words have rung down the years in my mind. He loved my mother; I'm quite sure of that. But, he said to me once in a moment of candor, "There is no one in the world I understand less than your mother." I am certain he meant that.

I want you to know then, that I reverence people for whom God is absent. I know full well that many religious people use the word "atheist" with disdain. Atheists are seen by some religious people as somehow irresponsible or lacking in honesty. I believe that is only rarely so. I believe that atheists are usually very honest people.[12] I reverence that. I am reminded of the profound mystery of absence that is such a part of real human friendship, almost a condition of deep human friendship; I reverence that too, for I know how easy it is to be in love and how hard it is later on when that feeling of absence is a counterplayer and a necessary part of friendships that perdure over the years. Lifelong friends always experience it. It is only the young ones, the newlyweds and the new converts who in their enthusiasm and ignorance find fault with those who know the meaning of absence.

I think of Teresa of Avila's sarcastic voice to God, "If this is how you treat your friends, no wonder you have so few!"[13] I think of the book of Job,[14] which is a book revered by Jews and Christians alike about God's absence from a just man. I think of the words of Jesus on the cross, "My God, my God, why have you forsaken me?"[15] The absence of God is not apart from either the Jewish or Christian tradition. It is there at the center.

It is clear to me that whether or not one discerns a godly presence in a field of purple, one can admire it. Whether or not one senses the divine in one's inner voices, one can still prepare to listen to them. What is the difference between a loving Christian or Jew and a loving agnostic or atheist? . . . in the light of the words:

God is love, and he who abides in love, abides in God and God in him.[16]

Surely we have made too much of the difference. Best to relegate the differences to small things. If a person is loving and honest, that person is near to God. I find it absurd to think that the author of love should reject anyone who practices love or that the author of truth should reject an honest person. I prefer to put the chief difference between atheists and believers down to the mystery of absence in friendship. And to add, that if you have really known friendship over a long period of time, whether human friendship or divine, you must perforce experience what it is to feel abandoned and alone.

Notes

[1]"No one has ever seen God." John 1/18.

In the encounter between Moses and God in the burning bush Gold refuses to give Moses his name. This refusal underlines the hidden nature of God to the Hebrew people. *The New Oxford Annotated Bible* (Revised Standard Version) (New York: Oxford University Press, 1973, 1977) p. 79, footnotes 13-15. Exodus 4/13-14.

[2]See Chapter Nine of the present text, "Prayer and Morality," footnote 14. Read carefully Martin Luther King's description of the inner voice which spoke to him.

[3]Part of the charm of the children's letters to God quoted in Chapter Two, "Childhood's Prayer," lies in the puzzlement of the kids over God's not responding to them with the same directness with which they write to him.

[4]Lawrence Ferlinghetti, *A Coney Island of the Mind* (New York: New Directions, 1958), p. 22. I might add that Ferlinghetti is a poet who writes about serious religious subjects in slang. If you like the poem quoted above, try #5, p. 15-16, #6, p. 17-18, "I am Waiting," pp. 49-53, "Christ Climbed Down," p. 69-70.

[5]Ignatius Loyola, *The Text of the Spiritual Exercises*, "Rules for the Discernment of Spirits for the Second Week," pp. 111-114.

[6]*Ibid.,* "Rules for the Discernment of Spirits for the First Week," XII, XIII, pp. 109-111. If you look up the Rules for Discernment, don't be put off by the warlike language or Ignatius' referring to the moods that come to one in prayer as from the good or bad angel. The message remains clear and practical. Only the images are out of date.

[7]It is basic to this quotation to see that in the dealings of persons with God the initiative is divine rather than human. So it was with the call of Moses (Exodus 3/1 ff.) as also the call of Abraham (Genesis 17/11 ff.) so it is when Christ himself was called: "He was led by the spirit into the wilderness." Matthew 4/1. This very basic notion is summed up well in the words, "You have not chosen me; I have chosen you." John 15/16.

[8]Erik Erikson writes tellingly of the power of the American work ethic, the American need to make things happen, *Toys and Reasons* (New York: Norton, 1977), p. 154.

Josef Pieper explores the shallowness of work without leisure. See *Leisure, the Basis of Culture* (New York: Pantheon, 1952), pp. 30-58.

[9]I want to underline here that love of any kind is a gift. We cannot force it or make it happen. We can only prepare for it; we can only accept it once given; we can only nourish it once present. See Irene Claremont de Castillejo, *Knowing Woman* (New York: Harper Colophon Books, 1973), Chapter VIII, "What do we Mean by Love?" pp. 116-117.

[10]Dorothy Day, one of the religious giants of modern America, reflected on her youth, before she became a Christian. In an interview with Robert Coles, she comments with compassion on her early friends and associates . . . "The longer I live, the more I see God at work in people who don't have the slightest interest in religion and never read the Bible and wouldn't know what to do if they were persuaded to go inside a church. I always knew how much I admired certain men and women (my 'radical friends') who were giving their lives to help others get a better break; but now I realize how spiritual some of them were, and I'm ashamed of myself for not realizing that long ago, when I was with them, talking and having supper and making our plans, as we did." Robert Coles, *Dorothy Day, A Radical Devotion* (Reading: Addison-Wesley, 1987). p. 29.

[11]Francis Kelly Nemeck and M.T. Coombs, *The Spiritual Journey* (Wilmington: Glazier, 1987), p. 175. See also John of the Cross, "The Spiritual Canticle," in *Collected Works,* p. 453-457. This would be a good time to reread Chapter Seven of *Searching for God,* "The Notion of God," especially the second half of the chapter.

[12]I once attended a lecture during the late nineteen sixties. The famous French Communist philosopher, Roger Garaudy was the speaker. Garaudy, the atheist, spoke so powerfully of the beauty of the world and the power of human love that I was deeply moved and at the same time upset. I was upset, because I had rarely heard a Christian speaker speak more forcefully than Garaudy. I had seldom heard anything so convincing or passionate from the pulpit of a church. I've never forgotten that speech.

Incidentally, since the talk was sponsored by a Roman Catholic institution, there was a great deal of public anger directed against the university for allowing a Communist to speak in a Catholic school. Father Paul Reinert, S.J., the president of St. Louis U. at the time, estimated the university lost at least a million dollars in donations, because of the anger of the university's benefactors over this "enemy of God" speaking at a university sponsored forum.

This would be an excellent time for the reader of this book to read *The Communist Manifesto* as an example of a profoundly spiritual book from an unlikely source. Not strange that Graham Greene, speaking in the mouth of one of his fictional characters, should find affinities between the *Manifesto* and The Sermon on the Mount from St. Matthew's gospel. Graham Greene, *Monsignor Quixote* (New York: Simon & Schuster, 1982), p. 97-107, 168. Karl Marx and Friedrich Engels, *The Communist Manifesto* (New York: Washington Square, 1964 [original German, 1848]).

[13]I have been unable to find a reference to this saying of Teresa's. Even if the saying is apocryphal, the words fit very well the frankness of Teresa's conversations with God and her fellow human beings.

[14]Even though the book of Job has a happy ending in its present form, it poses hard questions about the inevitable suffering that is the lot of even the best men and the best women. God has never been uniformly kind to good people.

[15]Matthew 27/46. Jesus is quoting Psalm 22. If you read the entire psalm, you will see that it is not a cry of despair alone, but the agonized call of one who is desperate, yet at the same time trusting God.

[16]1 John 3/7-13. The quote as I have used it, is a condensation of these verses.

11

Conversion

Some people do "find the answer." Some people have vivid experiences of God. Sometimes you can point to the very moment of discovery. I call such an experience a conversion. It is certainly possible to be a religious person without the drama of conversion, but it is equally possible to have a dramatic moment.[1] I want this chapter to be a guide for people who have recently had such an experience as well as a guide for people living with someone who has had such an experience recently.

Any big change brings with it problems of its own, even if the change is a good one. Social scientists have studied people who have gotten suddenly rich by winning the state lottery or a big prize in a quiz program or by an unexpected inheritance. Most big winners have had trouble adjusting to their good fortunes. It is naive to think that sudden good fortune means the same thing as having it made. I can remember Professor James Fowler of Emory University's Center for the Study of Faith Development remarking to me once that most people who have experienced a remarkable conversion get up the next morning expecting the world to be the same as it always was. Said Fowler, "After a conversion experience the world is never the same; your life is never the same. It will always be marked by that experience."[2]

I remember well the summer I was ordained a priest, twenty-five years ago. I had asked to be sent to a parish in Baltimore, Maryland, because that parish was one of the first Catholic parishes in the country to bring congregational singing into Sunday worship. The parish was mostly Black, mostly people who had left their own Protestant congregations for one reason or another and had joined the neighboring Catholic parish. These people had left their churches, but they hadn't left behind a tradition of congregational singing. Under the leadership of a priest not much older than myself they had gladly brought that singing tradition to the fore in a hitherto silent congregation.

The first Sunday I was there I was blown away by the music. It was altogether new to me; it was emotional; it was joyful and exuberant. I had experienced moments of quiet joy in church before but never exuberance. It was great! I felt positively carried off by the voices of those people. I fell in love with the whole congregation, moved as I was by their singing, their joy, and their cause. That summer the cause was civil rights as they concerned Black people; the parish was not only a singing parish; it was also a militant parish.

At the end of that summer I want back to Kansas to take my last year of theological training in the seminary. It was a very hard year, for I had a new vision, a new love. That vision and love were not shared by most of my professors and only by a handful of my fellow seminarians. I hadn't realized what it was like to have had a conversion and then to go on living the life back home. That year was a year of anger, impatience, and a sort of pervasive anxiety for me. I didn't lose my enthusiasm, but I frequently lost my cool and didn't sleep too well. A good number of my old friends found me to be a pain in the you-know-what. Nor did my friends and professors suddenly see the light that I had seen; I didn't make any converts, although I did find a few kindred spirits. Conversion is like that.

What if you have had a conversion experience? What if you are totally filled up with your religious discovery? Is there anything useful I can tell you?

First of all, no one can experience it for you. I believe there is an inevitable narrow focus that comes with sudden conversions.[3] I don't really expect you to believe me if I say that it will take you years to learn that your light is not the only light, no matter how bright it shines for you. I can hope, however, that in the years to come, the years in which you live out your revolution, you will very slowly become aware of the limitations of your vision as well as the goodness of the lives of other people who do not share your vision. At that point, when you are tempted to disillusionment, perhaps you will remember that your light can be a good one without necessarily being THE LIGHT of all time. That is a humbling experience, discovering that you are not the Messiah and that your people are not the only Chosen People. You will be a better person when you find that out, for you will know that your light is only one light among many and that your holy people are only one holy people among many. It is not a lesson learned easily or fast. It is the work of the rest of your life.

Enthusiasm and bigotry are very close to one another. You have experienced that by living with friends who are enthusiasts. Maybe you are rooming with a runner. The runner may think that all the world's problems would be solved if only everyone would run ten miles every day. Running is a marvelous activity, especially if one lives a sedentary life or is given to fits of depression. It has a wondrous cleansing quality; it can lift your spirits; it's good for your heart, your metabolism, and your soul. However, you may discover if you love running, that it tends to be very hard on your feet, your knees, and your back. You may even find out that there are other good ways of lifting your spirits and exercising your body. Even if they are not your way, they can be good ones. Long walks, playing golf, going fishing, climbing trees, gardening, back packing. The list is endless. Running isn't the only way. For some people it is a bad idea altogether, even if it is good for you. And runners, for all their virtues and soulfulness, are not the only good people in the world. If you despise the people of the world who are not runners, you are a bigot. A bigot is a narrow minded enthusiast.

To put it in religious terms, God is a very creative Father and Mother. God has many, many ways of drawing people. To be enthusiastic about the way God has chosen for you is beautiful. To refuse to believe that there are other ways is to shorten the arms of God; it is to say that your own image of the vastness of God is the only good one. There are many.

I would like to add here a reminder that you should be ready for the world staying much the same, even when you have changed. The next day when you get up will NOT be the same as the one before it. There will be hardship and misunderstanding; you should know that. Don't be surprised.

You might put it like this. After an experience of being knocked off your horse, as St. Paul was, you may well feel, "This is it!" or "I have been saved!" I am not here to dispute that, for I have had my own times of conversion and they are very precious to me. What I do want to say is this: just because you have seen the light does not mean that there is nothing further to do. It is possible even for converts to continue to grow. If you have had a conversion experience, your life isn't over; it is just beginning.

There is a good analogy with love. If you fall in love with someone, you may think, "This is it! I've never been blown away like this before." You may regard your mother and father with pity, because it seems to you that they are far removed in their relationship from the overpowering beauty of your own. I'd never deny the beauty of being in love; it's an incredible experience. To say that it is a high point of your life may well be true, but you have a lot of life to come yet. Love can grow and deepen in the years ahead. It can die too, of course. So, you have to nourish it; you have to sweat with it; you have to be willing to experience times when you don't feel it at all.[4] Usually you have to get to know the person you are in love with and still find that person loveable. It really is easier to be in love, when you don't know your loved one very well. Your love is a lot deeper when you know someone very well and still love her.

Falling in love is like the conversion experience. It is the beginning of love, not the end. There is a lot to happen between you and your newly discovered God. It would be a tragedy for you to think this adventure is over when in point of fact you have just begun. It would surely be selling your tradition short. There's more to it that the first magic moment.

A word on enthusiasm again, from a different point of view. I think that one of the traps lying in wait for people who have made a great discovery lies in unknowingly forgetting what they have discovered.[5]

Suppose you have a great love of books. You talk books all the time. You even get a job in a bookstore selling books. You love selling books. It's great! You get so wrapped up in selling that you no longer have time to read. Slowly your enthusiasm begins to fade, because it is not nourished by reading, until you become a sort of empty salesperson. There is a kind of enthusiasm on the outside but nothing on the inside. Your enthusiasm either fades or becomes fake and artificial. You suffer from burnout. If you are religious, you take the chance of becoming the very two-faced person you once abhorred.

I want to add that I think most converts have this experience. It's not so much that you should avoid it as that when it happens, you recognize it. Then you need to go back quietly to the roots of your conversion and see to it that your enthusiasm gets nourishment, even if that nourishment takes time away from spreading the word. The basic nourishment for all religious enthusiasm is prayer and prayerful reading. Making time for it is just as necessary as reading is for a bookseller or a teacher.

The real test of any conversion is the life that follows from it. You test your conversion with living. If you become deeper, if you become more loving and more tolerant, your time of change is authenticated. "By their fruits you shall know them," as the gospel says. That is the only worthwhile test.

Now, let's put the shoe on the other foot. Suppose you are the roommate or friend of someone who has had a religious conversion. Is there anything you should know that might be helpful to you?

What do you do about this sudden rush of enthusiasm in a person you liked the way she was, before all this change? I think it only honest to say that there is a good chance you may have to cool it for a while. You may find that your enthusiastic friend doesn't want to listen to your objections or your differences. You may find that your old buddy who was once a good listener is a good listener no more. Don't panic; your old friend will cool down eventually. I don't think a lot of heated argument is useful. It can drive you apart; it can make you both bitter. You may have to distance yourself from your friend for a while, or you may have the disconcerting experience of your friend doing it for you. I suggest that YOU may have to be the tolerant one, as unfair as that may seem. You very likely will have to be patient; enthusiasts can be exasperating. If your friendship really does have substance, it will survive; but you will have to wait. It may mean not being roommates next semester during the settling down period. And of course, it is possible that your friendship was not as deep as you thought. If that's really true, it's good to find out, no matter how painful it is. But, give it some time; it will be a while before you know.

It is certainly fair for you to be concerned about your friend. We both know that there really are some destructive conversions. There really are some brands of religion which have little to recommend them. Bad religion can be very destructive. We'd better talk about some signs of a false conversion, so that you may have something to go on in assessing your friend's newfound way of life. To begin with, it is possible that your friend has been deceived. It's good to know that. I'm going to offer you some signs of bad conversions.

I don't think it is unhealthy for a person's religious life to be all-devouring, given the fact that a honeymoon is perfectly normal both in love and religion. What is *not* normal is that the all encompassing nature of early love remain pervasive. If your friend joins a group of people whose only friends are other church members, that's not good. It isn't a good sign if the body of believers are ingrown either. What do I mean by that? Social scientists use the term "total institution." A total institution is ingrown. The members all go to each other's shops, listen to each other's music, are of one mind in politics. They take their recreation with other "members" only; they eat only with one another. To put it briefly, they are so convinced of the authenticity of their religion that they think everyone outside will contaminate them as true believers. Ideas of outsiders are just as suspect as social contact. The total institution is a law unto itself and will not tolerate contact with the outside world.

What's the danger? Why not be a member of a total institution, especially if it is within that institutional framework that you had your conversion experience? I can see nothing against living in such a way as such. My problem lies with what you call "side effects." We live in a pluralistic society here in the United States. If we avoid contact with those not like ourselves, there is a terrible danger of narrowness. I do not mean of course that people who belong to the same church should not socialize. Your family is not a bad family just because the people in it cherish their times together. By no means, those times together are vital to a family's vibrancy just as times together with people who share your beliefs are vital to the health of your religious life.

The problem lies with the exclusion of outsiders and outside ideas as threatening your way of life.

I can recall someone telling me once that the Arapaho Indians living in Wyoming would be best served by the rest of the American people if we would leave them to themselves.[6] After all, American white folks have done terrible things to Native Americans. Everybody knows that. I should like to add that it does nobody any good just to wring their hands about the past. The Arapaho and the Whites around them as a matter of fact are there. Neither group can pretend that they live in a different age without suffering terrible harm. If you are an Indian you'd better know how to drive a pickup truck. You'd better know how to deal with cattle buyers, traveling salesmen, TV advertisements, whiskey, highways, and people who would like to buy your land. No amount of wishing is going to keep the modern world off the reservation. If the Indian people try to hide from the outside world, that world will grind them up and spit them out without mercy. It is as important that Arapaho Indians understand the white world around them as it is for the white folks to understand the Indian. We have only one world between us. If you are an Indian, hiding from it is one of the best ways of ensuring that you will get cheated when it comes time to sell your cattle, that you will get bamboozled by traveling salesmen, drunk on the white man's whiskey, killed on his highways, seduced by his TV ads, and coerced into losing your land.

It makes no more sense to live in a totally enclosing religious group than it does for Indians to try to pretend that they can live without contact with the world they are a part of.

The outside world can act as a corrective to abuses within the more intimate one. Outside ideas are the source of fair criticism within. There are some good ideas and some good people out there. If you try to avoid the outside world you will be at one and the same time at the mercy of unscrupulous people within your congregation and predators on the outside. I suppose the real bottom line is this: The world we live in is impossible to exclude it. We're stuck with it. We'd better understand it or it will hurt us. It has been wisely said that the only viable total institutions left in our world are hospitals for the incurably insane, people who are incapable of functioning in the outside world. I am going to presume that the members of your new church are not crazy and that they can function on the outside as adults. If the church presumes otherwise, it makes children out of adults. Adults who act like children are not healthy people. That brings up another issue, the issue of authority. Every institution, every organization, every country exercises authority. Authority goes with government; you can't do without it in your church any more than you can do without it in your country. I hope neither you nor I have any kick against some kind of authority in every organization. Authority can be misused too. Americans have an almost inborn distrust of absolute authority, for we have governed our country in a government by the people, of the people, and for the people from our beginnings as a nation. We are proud of our heritage of being a democratic country and we should be. We know that every few years we get a chance to choose a new president and a new congress. Our representatives have to do a good job or we replace them. We respect the authority of our government, but we don't bow down before it. We certainly don't worship it.

By the same token church authority is as human as government authority. No matter how legitimate the authorities of a church are, those authorities are not God.[7] Your church is an organization to help you know, love and serve God. I think it is very important to know that your church is a helper, a very human helper. Absolute authority lies with God, not the church. We worship God rather than the church. So far, so good?

The kicker is that it frequently happens that church leaders have a way of slipping themselves into God's place. If a church organization demands unthinking obedience from its members, the organization is trying to be God. Church members obviously should respect the authority of their church and their tradition. Respect and worship are not the same thing. There is a bottom line in everyone's life that goes beyond any church authority. That bottom line is a person's conscience. I have to be honest with myself in my service of God. If there is a serious conflict between my church and my conscience, I have no recourse in my service of God but to be as honest as I can, to do what I think is right. All human authority has limitations and this includes church authority.

If you are concerned about your roommate or friend's newfound faith, ask what kind of obedience her church asks of her. Cults are religious organizations which demand unquestioning obedience to human church leaders.[8] The followers of the Reverend Jim Jones drank poisoned cups of Coca-Cola because he ordered it. The result was tragedy. You don't want your friend to be a member of a cult. If the group has a name, you can check with the campus minister. Campus ministers almost always are aware of cults on campus; they themselves are not likely to be dictators; universities are very leary of having absolutists as campus ministers.

I might add that it isn't easy to rescue someone from a cult. Sometimes all you can do is recognize cults for what they are so that you yourself will not make the same mistake as your friend.

A couple of other danger signs to look for in a convert friend are radical personality change and sudden, violent conversion. I realize that there can be authentic change that is dramatic and fast, but I do suggest that you tread warily for a while if you have a friend who undergoes a sudden religious change. For every genuine sudden conversion there are plenty that are brought about by unscrupulous leaders, by deception, by out and out flimflam. Time is the best test.

Sudden radical personality change is not a good sign either, granted that plenty of new converts "get religion" for a while and become a pain to their old friends. Real religion is characterized by genuine concern for other people, by real compassion, by a willingness to listen.[9]

Fanatics just want you to join their group; they are often not really concerned about you; they usually don't listen to you, except where it serves their purposes, and they rarely respect your conscience and dignity as a person. If your friend suddenly becomes a fanatic, show him compassion yourself, but know there is something drastically wrong.

The good Spirit, as we have noted before, brings calm and peace; it is not a flash in the pan; it lasts. It is prayerful.[10] Far from trying to manipulate other people; it respects them.

As I close this section on conversion I want you to know that I have drawn it with broad strokes. There are very few real cults; there are very few total fanatics. At the same time I don't know of any churches that have no fanatics in them. I think the number of ministers that escape temptations to play God are few. Playing God is an occupational hazard for priests, rabbis and ministers. The best of them fall for it sometimes. In the real world, good and bad religion is generally mixed up in the same church, the same people, and the same conversion experience.

What sane religious people hope for is a church that is more loving than fanatic, ministers who are more compassionate than arrogant, people who are more caring than narrow, who have within themselves the seeds of love and intelligence along with unreasoned enthusiasm and bigotry. All human life is a mixed bag. I hope neither one of us ever forgets that.

Notes

[1]The conversion of St. Paul is perhaps the most celebrated dramatic religious change of heart in Western religious history. Acts 9/1-9.

[2]James Fowler, *Stages in Faith,* pp. 274-275. Fowler speaks of such changes as "painful and dislocating." I know of no better description of the process of conversion that that of William James. See *The Varieties of Religious Experience,* Lectures Eight to Ten (New York: Modern Library, 1902), pp. 163-253.

[3]Erik Erikson's treatment of "ideology" is instructive concerning the process of conversion in youth. See *Young Man Luther,* pp. 40-47.

[4]I refer the reader to the description of maturing love in Chapter Seven of the present work, "The Notion of God." Erich Fromm has a good description of mature love in *The Art of Loving* (New York: Bantam, 1956), pp. 14-18.

[5]Teresa of Avila tells of her discovery of the kind of prayer we have explained in Chapters Three, Four and Six. It was a great revelation to her, a freeing experience. She became so enthusiastic about it that she sought to share her discovery with other people, including her father. Such was her enthusiasm that she gradually abandoned the practice of meditation while spending more and more time trying to get other people to practice it. "Vida," Chapter Seven, #10-12, *Collected Works, Volume One,* pp. 59-61.

[6]Margaret Craven tells a story of an anthropologist who wanted a group of Indians in Canada's Pacific Northwest to remain forever untouched by the white man's world. The story illustrates the futility of such a wish. *I Heard the Owl Call My Name* (New York: Dell, 1973), pp. 102-105.

[7]Erich Fromm describes well how authority can become an idol. One can worship church authority in place of worshipping God. See *Psychoanalysis and Religion* (New York: Bantam, 1950), pp. 34-37.

[8]Erich Fromm uses term "incest" to describe an overly dependent relationship between an individual and her religious group. Incest, as Fromm uses the term, is at the heart of cult membership. *Psychoanalysis and Religion*, p. 77-85.

[9]William James, *The Varieties of Religious Experience,* pp. 320-331.

[10]See Chapter Ten of the present work, "The Problem of Unbelief," especially the section on how to tell a true inner voice from a false one.

12

A Question of Content

After a discussion of conversions, someone is bound to ask, "Why are you spending all this time talking about how God speaks and the challenges of conversion without ever talking about WHAT the beliefs are to which a person could be converted?" We're back to our old problem of not being able to say everything at once. Logically, the question of the contents of belief should occur very early in a discussion of searching for God.

Indeed we have talked about what kind of a being God is; that is the most basic question of belief, but I grant you, there are lots of others.

You could look on what you believe as a sort of divine checklist.[1] If you believe the right things, then you go to heaven; if you don't, you go to hell. That is, if you believe in heaven and if you believe in hell. In any case, you could look at belief as a kind of loyalty oath to God.

When you were a child, you heard the stories of tradition, taking them pretty literally as children do.[2] You probably liked the ones with a lot of action in them. A couple of children's letters to God will explain what I mean:

> Dear God,
>   Your book has a lot of zip to it.
>   I like science fiction stories.
>   You had very good ideas and I would like to
>   know where you found them.
>
>   —Your reader
>   Jimmy

Here's another one.

> Dear God,
> We are learning about Jonah and the Whale,
> Where he swallowed him and everything. It is
> the best story I ever heard with action and
> fright. My daddy says it sounds pretty fishy.
> Do you think that's funny.
>
> > —Very truly,
> > Sidney.

Yet one more.

> Dear God,
> My teacher read us the part where all the jews
> went through where the water was and got away.
> Keep up the good work. I am jewish.
>
> > —Love
> > Paula[3]

I'm sure you get the idea. That sense of wonder we talked about in an earlier chapter, the love of a good story, and of course, a heavy dose of self-interest.

What happens later, rather gradually, beginning roughly with your teen years, is that you begin to question those stories. You ask what they mean. You want to know if they are historically true. You wonder if they have any religious meaning.

I can recall my disillusionment long after my teenaged years when I first asked myself what the basic Christian notion of three persons in one God meant to me. Father, Son, and Holy Spirit . . . three persons: one God. I wondered which of the three to pray to. I wondered how there could be three persons and one God. I wondered why Jesus never said he was God in the New Testament. I had learned to explain the Trinity as a shamrock . . . three leaves, one shamrock. Well, that no longer made sense to me.[4] I was smart enough to know that each leaf is not a shamrock, only the three of them on a stem. I had to admit that the three-in-one stuff didn't mean much to me. I didn't spend a lot of time on it; I just prayed to God and let somebody else sort out which one of the three I was praying to.

Years later, I heard a sermon on the Trinity. The clergyman giving the sermon said that there were an awful lot of ways of looking at such a large being as God. Three of those ways are as follows: I could look at God as a loving Father. That could be helpful. I could look upon the person of Jesus as God, present somehow in a very special human being. I could look at the presence of God in the world as the Holy Spirit. The preacher freely admitted that there were many other ways of looking at God. God is referred to many ways in Jewish and Christian scriptures: as a warrior, as a lover, as a mother, as an outraged spouse whose wife has deserted him, as a potter working in clay.[5]

Those are just a few. We have spoken about most of these in Chapter Seven of this book. There are a lot more ways to speak of God too. The three of the Trinity have a special place in Christian tradition.

I know as well that beliefs in any tradition can become the personal property of a small group of church officials who can use them as a test for orthodoxy or, worse yet, as a sort of sterile intellectual playground far removed from the ordinary people or from the experiential sources in which they had their origin.

Let me explain. I remember thinking once during my theological studies as a young Jesuit that we were occupying ourselves with such vital questions as how many angels could dance on the head of a needle. Who cares? Who cares whether the Holy Spirit proceeds from the Father and the Son? Who cares just exactly how Jesus was God and man? Who cares if Mary was really a virgin or just symbolically so?

Wars have been fought on all of these subjects. People HAVE cared at one time or another. What I want to say is that all religious beliefs are distillations of centuries of religious experience, centuries of prayer.[6]

Frequently the answer to the question "Who cares?" may be quite startling. It's as though there is deep meaning in most old beliefs if we are willing to take the time to use our own categories today to mine the meaning.

Let's take the example of the Holy Spirit. Who cares about the third person of the Trinity? Wouldn't two persons be enough? Let's do some digging.

Contemporary writers have looked at the context in which the word "spirit" is used in the Old Testament and find that the symbolism is *feminine!*[7] The door has been opened to see, right at the heart of the Hebrew scriptures as well as Christian scriptures, an image of God more motherly than fatherly, more feminine than masculine. In a world where women's roles have changed so much it is astounding to find central female imagery in such traditional expressions of the godhead as the Spirit. The Spirit is a motherly image of God.

By the same token, the Roman Catholicism's traditional reverence for the person of Mary, the mother of Jesus, has been seen by many moderns as nothing short of idolatry and superstition. Latin Catholics have especially been laughed at, for their respect for the virgin seems to eclipse the reverence due to the Godhead.[8]

How fascinating to hear C.G. Jung congratulate Catholicism for keeping the feminine image of God alive through the reverence of Mary.[9] Jung takes Reformation Christians to task for having a God who seems exclusively masculine, who is a judge more than a lover, who is concerned for cold principles rather than the interrelationships of the nitty gritty of ordinary life.[10]

Carol Gilligan and other contemporary psychologists have noted that women often concern themselves with interrelationships and compassion for the individual, whereas men frequently concern themselves exclusively with principles and logic when it comes to questions of value.[11] How interesting to discover that the person of Mary keeps the feminine side of the godhead alive. How interesting to see the Holy Spirit as a feminine image of God. Both are correctives to a notion of God which is overly masculine and warlike, a cold, analytical God, lacking in compassion and mercy. The seed of this modern insight was there all along in two ancient beliefs: the doctrine of the Spirit and the ancient reverence for the Virgin Mary.

I myself have found it interesting to read the book of Jonah with an eye cocked to the writer's intention rather than getting bogged down in the controversy as to whether a person could live for three days in the belly of a large fish,[12] avoiding an endless discussion about whether there were indeed any fish (or whales) large enough to swallow a grown man in the Mediterranean Sea of biblical times.

The *point* of the story is that God asked Jonah, a Hebrew, to preach to some people who were NOT his people, who were not Hebrews, who were not THE CHOSEN PEOPLE. Jonah didn't want to have anything to do with outsiders. He knew his own people were the Chosen Ones. All the others must be bad guys. That is a modern problem as well as an ancient one. Many modern religious people see their own group as THE ONLY group; they want nothing to do with outsiders. We have discussed that in the last chapter in the context of conversion, as well as in other contexts in this book. People who think their own group is the only legitimate one are almost always bigots. Bigotry is as common today as it was in Jonah's time.

Because Jonah didn't want to have anything to do with preaching to outsiders, in this case the people of the city of Nineveh, he jumped aboard a ship bound for what is today called Spain. The sailors on board ship discovered the stowaway during a terrible storm. They thought he was bad luck to them. They thought his presence was somehow connected to the storm, so they pitched him overboard. At this point Jonah is swallowed by a huge fish. The fish vomits up poor old Jonah onto the shore outside the very city he was trying to avoid.

Jonah gets the message. He realizes he can't escape, so he preaches to all the people of Nineveh; he tells them to mend their ways and to do penance for all the bad things they have done. To his great surprise, the Ninevites, right down to and including their cattle, listen carefully to him. They decide to mend their ways. They even put on the traditional sackcloth garment of sorrow and cover their heads with ashes. Jonah is not happy with his success. He wants his bad guys to continue to be bad guys. He sits under a fig tree and pouts about this revolting turn of events. The Lord himself has to speak to him, explaining that outsiders, in this case the people of Nineveh, are dear to Him as well as the Chosen People of the Hebrew Nation. This is a story about the love of God for all people, written in protest to a very narrow view of a loving God. It is as relevant today as it was more than two thousand years ago, when it was written. It would be too bad to get hung up in a big argument (as Christians have done for years) over whether one had to literally believe that a man was swallowed by a large fish or not. The point of this ancient story is much more important.

My point is simply this. We need to examine old beliefs and the stories of scripture with new eyes, looking for the gems of religious truth hidden in them rather than getting lost in controversy built around using the literal truth of such things as a measure of whether one is a good Christian or a good Jew. We need to get under the surface and see these inspired stories as evidence of the religious experience of our ancestors in faith. In the case of our discussion of Mary and the Spirit, to see that at its root, there is reason to see God under the image of woman, with the warmth, compassion and flexibility that such an image calls forth. In the case of the story of Jonah we can see clear evidence for a God who loves and calls all people, and not just one group.

I have given you two examples, but there are many more. Those inspired stories and beliefs have lasted a long time; frequently there is much more to them than meets the eye. This process is not entirely different from admiring a "field of purple." A person must have a sense of openness is both cases, a sense of wonder, a dimension of living which is unhurried, at least some of the time.

I should like to add here a sort of connective between the beliefs, so often summarized in Creeds and commandments, between the great inspired stories of scripture, and the present day. If you really do think of the Spirit as brooding over the world as it is pictured in one of the creation stories of Genesis,[13] it is well to realize that the Spirit still broods over the world, and has from the moment of the beginnings until now. The poet Hopkins puts it well. Commenting on how worn and battered our world has become at the hands of humankind he notes that:

> . . . all is seared with trade; bleared, smeared with toil;
> And wears man's smudge and shares man's smell; the soil
>
> Is bare now, nor can foot feel, being shod.

But then he notes the presence of the Spirit:

> And for all this, nature is never spent;
> There lives the dearest freshness deep down things;
>
> And though the last lights off the black West went
> Oh, morning, at the brown brink eastward, springs—
>
> Because the Holy Ghost over the bent
> World broods with warm breast and with ah! bright wings.[14]

I think it is important to see, with the poet, that the Spirit of God is still brooding over the world. In particular, I am concerned that we see God's presence in many other ways than old creeds and ancient scriptures. That's the general point of the many quotes throughout this book about admiring Alice Walker's "field of purple." Furthermore, see the presence of God in modern ways of knowing. We need to put the insights and culture of our own day to work on our ancient traditions. Let's see if I can explain to you what I mean.

The belief of heaven has been justly criticized by Karl Marx, because he noted that sometimes churches have told poor people to be content with their lot, citing heaven as a reason.[15] The idea being not to worry about having a bad life here in this world, because God will reward you in the next world. This is a neat way of using a religious belief to justify employers not paying a fair wage. It lines up the churches, especially church officers, with the rich and powerful against those who have little influence and little money. There's a beautiful example of an evil way to use a traditional belief.

Heaven is an old idea;[16] it exists in various forms in Judaism's later books, in Christianity, in Islam, and Hinduism. Is there another way of looking at it?

Contemporary scientists are fascinated with the idea of new and undiscovered worlds. They are interested in other galaxies, other dimensions, other spaces. They are dead serious about this too.[17] It takes great imagination and great courage to reason about such things and to look for them. How very strange that most religions have been serious about other worlds for centuries. The little kid whose letter I quoted wasn't far off when he said in writing to God, "Your book has a lot of zip to it. I like science fiction stories."[18] Only in our own day do we see that religion's concern with other worlds has come to touch upon the same concern among physicists and astronomers. The idea of another world and another life need not be used as an excuse to be unfair to people in want. It can be a source of hope, a source of wonder to all of us.

The idea of creation is an old idea too. It certainly goes back before the days when the Hebrew people came across it in Babylon and incorporated it into their own book of Genesis.[19] And yet the creation story has been sometimes interpreted as God making the world in six days and then letting it run like a top, on its own.

Darwin and the evolutionists who have come after him, have seen a more dynamic creation process, even if they do not use that word.[20] In the process of slow change and development, the world is always being created anew. The hand of the Creator is seen with modern eyes as always present in this growing and changing world. The original insight of God as creator is seen to be just the seed of a more comprehensive creator, a creator always at work, always present to the universe. To repeat Hopkins' lines, "the Holy Ghost over the bent/World broods with warm breast and with ah! bright wings."

It is our own times and our own knowledge that have given us eyes to see the intimacy with which the creator is present in the world's evolutionary process.[21] An old belief, and old inspired story, takes on new meaning in the present day.

So, I have given you a small taste of what a modern person can do with finding meaning in old stories and old faith formulations. The very age of these stories and formulations is evidence that there is a lot there if you are willing to look. They have lasted through many ages, because people found meaning in them at various times. They are the great themes of the relationship between God and humankind. They come up again and again in each age in a new form for people to rediscover. Your task and mine is to realize that there is much there in the content of scriptures and old creeds if we are willing to take the time to use our own modern insights on those old and resonant songs of love.

THAT is why content is important. The beliefs of faith are the echoes of God's presence to people over the millenia. They are based on the encounter between our ancestors and God, which is what I call prayer. Look at them again with your own new eyes and over the years you will find much treasure in them, much to add to your store of wonder, a new and historical dimension to your "field of purple."

Notes

[1] I might add that the "checklist" approach smacks of what Erich Fromm calls Authoritarian Religion. The lists, after all, are made up by human beings. It's not hard to see that the listmakers could be prone to making themselves little gods. See *Psychoanalysis and Religion*, p. 33-36 and p. 83.

[2] *Searching for God*, Chapter Two, "Childhood's Prayer."

[3] *Children's Letters to God*, no pagination in the book.

[4] Frank Sheed, the English theologian and publisher, is reported to have called much of what passed under the name of theological studies, "theometry." Theometry being an amalgam of geometry and the study of God. The Shamrock approach to the Trinity is in this category.

[5] I want here to give the reader a reference or two from the scriptures alluded to. I will take each theme separately.

Warrior. Read from the books of Exodus, Joshua and Judges for a clear picture of the warrior God of the early days of the Hebrew people.

Lover. The Song of Songs is especially relevant here. See also Hosea 2/21 and Jeremiah 31/20, 22.

Mother. See Isaiah 66/13 and 49/15 for images of God as mother.

Spouse. Isaiah 54/5 and Hosea 1-3.

Potter. Genesis 2/4-25 pictures the creation as done by a potter-God working in clay.

I refer the reader to the *Vocabulaire de Theologie Biblique* (Paris: Editions du Cerf, 1964). See themes of "Guerre," "Amour," "Mere," "Epoux," and "Creation."

[6]C.J. Jung, *Psychology and Religion,* (New Haven: Yale, 1938), p. 56-63.

[7]John Farrelly, *God's Work in a Changing World,* (Lanham: U. Press of America, 1985), p. 49-76.

[8]Frederico Fellini, *La Dolce Vita* (Mt. Vernon, New York: Audio Brandon Films, 1961). This film gives the viewer a taste of the Latin enthusiasm for Mary the mother of Jesus. I refer the reader, in a different context to the New Mexican author, Fra Angelico Chavez for a large number of books about the virgin in the piety of Mexican-American people.

[9]C.G. Jung, *Memories, Dreams, Reflections* (New York: Vantage Books, 1961), p. 201-202.

[10]*Ibid.*, p. 202.

[11]Carol Gilligan, *In a Different Voice* (Cambridge: Harvard, 1982), p. 24-63. Mary Belenky *et al., Women's Ways of Knowing* (New York: Basic Books, 1986), p. 8-9.

[12]*The New Oxford Annotated Bible,* "The Book of Jonah," (New York: Oxford, 1977), p. 1120.

[13]Genesis 1/2.

[14]This poem is quoted in its entirety in Appendix B of this book.

[15]Karl Marx, *Critique of Hegel's Philosophy of Right* (Cambridge: Cambridge U. Press, 1970 [original German, 1844]), pp. 131-132. Joe Hill, martyr to the cause of American labor and song writer, echoed Marx well when he has a preacher in a satirical song say, "you'll get pie in the sky when you die." Gibbs M. Smith, *Joe Hill* (Salt Lake City: U. of Utah Press, 1969), p. 233.

[16]John Hick, *Death and Eternal Life* (New York: Harper and Row, 1984), p. 171-159. Hans King, *Eternal Life?* (Garden City: Doubleday, 1984), p. 54-56

[17]Carl Sagan's novel, *Contact,* dramatizes this theme of interest in other worlds. Sagan, of course, is an astronomer. *Contact* (New York: Simon and Schuster, 1985).

[18]Eric Marshall and Stuart Hample, *Children's Letters to God.*

[19]*Vocabulaire de Theologie Biblique,* "Creation," p. 171.

[20]Charles Darwin, *The Origin of the Species and the Descent of Man* (New York: Modern Library, 1959), p. 374.

[21]Pierre Teilhard de Chardin, *The Divine Milieu,* (New York, Harper and Row, 1960) [original French, 1957], pp. 13, 66.

13

Conclusions

We are coming to the end. I want to summarize this book and remind you of its limitations. I want to remind you that the bedrock for a good reading of these chapters is your own honesty. It is a bad idea to try to fake religious conviction (except, perhaps, once in a while to please your mother while you are still making up your mind). If the task of youth is to find something worth being faithful to, this is not the time for faking it.

Basic to this book is that prayer forms the cornerstone of any religious search. Prayer is the foundation without which all the philosophy and religious reasoning in the world cannot stand. It is born of a sense of wonder and stillness both outside and inside a person, without which a person cannot appreciate the world, let alone the world's author.

Also basic to this book is to examine your own religious tradition before you choose another, or none. This book has been written in the heartfelt belief that there are many good religious traditions and many good religious congregations. It is more important to find a good tradition with truth in it than it is to find the best tradition or all the truth.

If one is to search for God, one must look both outside and inside one's self. We all use anthropomorphic images of God. Let us discern which of these images better lend themselves to a faith that is adult and giving. If one is to search for God, it is well to look in all the various moments of human living, in high times and low times, and above all, in ordinary times. For it is in ordinary times that we spend the vast majority of our lifetimes.

In looking for a congregation with which to share our faith, if faith we have, it is well to look for a people who are simply good or fitting. Looking for the best is perilous; hoping to find only upright people in any congregation is foolish. All congregations contain good and bad people; all people contain within themselves good and evil. A people can help one share a tradition, as long as one knows that the people are not God. They are not even Godlike all the time. We should never confuse a people with God. They should help us get to God and we should help them do the same.

And morality? Good and evil choices? What is its rock bottom? The foundation of all morality is human caring. The chief fruit of all prayer is a more caring person. There is much truth in the aphorism: "Love and do what you will." It is clear from experience that there are loving agnostics. It is equally clear that everyone with a good mind is in some sense an agnostic. That there are caring atheists in the world is a matter that is obvious to anyone who cares to have open eyes. It is very perilous to judge the motivation of anyone who does not believe in God, since we have all been admonished, "Judge not and ye shall not be judged." It is a simple fact of history that God has chosen to remain hidden from many people of integrity and intelligence. At the same time, if "God is love," those of us who are only occasionally loving need not fear that the great Lover won't be able to find a way to bring those who do not hear her voice to herself.

There are certain things you should know about conversion, whether your own or that of a friend. Conversions can be very good things or very bad things; often they are, especially at the beginning, a mixture of both.

As for the content of your tradition, if you have chosen a good tradition, its content will be very old. It is basically the results of the prayer of those who went before you in your tradition down through the centuries. You will need to ponder these old stories and beliefs in tune with your own times to find the beauty and truth that lies within them, the way a kernel of wheat lies hidden in its husk.

It is this author's belief that in all your times and places of searching you will not be alone. In the last analysis, whatever you find will be more a matter of being found than of finding. An old song is here apropos:

I once was lost, but now I'm found, was bound but now I'm free.

The End of the Book

but not

The End of the Journey

Postscript

One of the readers of the manuscript for this book expressed dismay that a book entitled *Searching for God* should have, as he put it, "no theological content." If college students are embarking on an intellectual quest of one kind or another, one would expect to find in a book such as this one, some reference to the great theoretical thinkers who have concerned themselves with studying God and God's dealings with us people of earth.

I would like to underline by way of response to the reader mentioned above that it is my settled conviction that the heart of religion is *not* theoretical; the heart of religion is the meeting of man or woman with God. I have compared contact with God to human friendship in this book. I believe that analogy is an apt one.

Psychologists, anthropologists, sociologists, philosophers and theologians have speculated about friendship down the ages. So have poets, playwrights, and the writers of song. It is possible to learn a great deal about friendship from theoreticians.

I should like to emphasize here that the rock bottom of friendship is not theory at all. It cannot be learned out of a book or in a class. People who have little education do have friends. Illiterates have friends.

Friendship is not something experienced primarily by the very intelligent or the highly educated. Educated people have indeed found help in understanding their loved ones and the processes of friendship by studying theoretical materials which attempt to analyze the process.

No theory however, makes the matter of the school of hard knocks superfluous. Friendship's fundament is now and always has been experience. You learn it primarily by bumping into other people. There is no substitute. The encounter between persons is first in importance and first in time in the business of knowing, loving and caring for others.

I need not defend the primacy of encounter in making friends. It is obvious. However, it is often *not* so obvious that the school of hard knocks and the business of encounter is just as surely the bedrock of a person's relationship with God.

Intellectuals often think that they can reason their way into religious conviction. It is the main underlying theme of this book that one must begin with experience when speaking about God. The first steps in faith are experiential; experience remains the heart of faith from birth to death.

Appendix A

Selection from
The Color Purple

Dear Nettie,

I don't write to God no more, I write to you.

What happen to God? ast Shug.

Who that? I say.

She look at me serious.

Big a devil as you is, I say, you not worried bout no God, surely.

She say, Wait a minute. Hold on just a minute here.

Just because I don't harass it like some peoples us know don't mean I ain't got religion.

What God do for me? I ast.

She say, Celie! Like she shock. He gave you life, good health, and a good woman that love you to death.

Yeah, I say, and he give me a lynched daddy, a crazy mama, a low-down dog of a step pa and a sister I probably won't ever see again. Anyhow, I say, the God I been praying and writing to is a man. And act just like all   the other mens I know. Trifling, forgitful and lowdown.

She say, Miss Celie, You better hush. God might hear you.

Let 'im hear me, I say. If he ever listened to poor colored women the world would be a different place. I can tell you.

She talk and she talk, trying to budge me way from blasphemy. But I blaspheme much as I want to.

All my life I never care what people thought bout nothing I did, I say. But deep in my heart I care about God. What he going to think. And come to find out, he don't think. Just sit up there glorying in being deef, I reckon. But it ain't easy, trying to do without God. Even if you know he ain't there, trying to do without him is a strain.

I is a sinner, say Shug. Cause I was born. I don't deny it. But once you find out what's out there waiting for us, what else can you be?

Sinners have more good times, I say.

You know why? she ast.

Cause you ain't all the time worrying bout God, I say.

Naw, that ain't it, she say. Us worry bout God a lot. But once us feel loved by God, us do the best us can to please him with what us like.

You telling me God love you, and you ain't never done nothing for him? I mean, not go to church, sing in the choir, feed the preacher and all like that?

But if God love me, Celie, I don't have to do all that. Unless I want to. There a lot of other things I can do that I speck God likes.

Like what? I ast.

Oh, she say. I can lay back and just admire stuff. Be happy. Have a good time.

Well, this sound like blasphemy sure nuff.

She say, Celie, tell the truth, have you ever found God in church? I never did. I just found a bunch of folks hoping for him to show. Any God I ever felt in church I brought in with me. And I think all the other folks did too. They come to church to SHARE God, not fin God.

Some folks didn't have him to share, I said. They the ones didn't speak to me while I was there struggling with my big belly and Mr. __'s children.

Right, she say.

Then she say: Tell me what your God look like, Celie.

Aw naw, I say. I'm too shame. Nobody ever ast me this before, so I'm sort of took by surprise. Besides, when I think about it, it don't seem quite right. But it all I got. I decide to stick up for him, just to see what Shug say.

Okay, I say. He big and old and tall and graybearded and white. He wear white robes and go barefooted.

Blue eyes? she ast.

Sort of bluish-gray. Cool. Big though. White lashes, I say.

She laugh.

Why you laugh? I ast. I don't think it so funny. What you expect him to look like, Mr.___?

That wouldn't be no improvement, she say. Then she tell me this old white man is the same God she used to see when she prayed. If you wait to find God in church, Celie, she say, that's who is bound to show up, cause that's where he live.

How come? I ast.

Cause that's the one that's in the white folks' white bible.

Shug! I say. God wrote the bible, white folks had nothing to do with it.

How come he look just like them, then? she say. Only bigger? And a heap more hair. How come the bible just like everything else they make, all about them doing one thing and another, and all the colored folks doing is gitting cursed?

I never thought bout that.

Nettie say somewhere in the bible it say Jesus' hair was like lamb's wool, I say.

Well, say Shug, if he came to any of these churches we talking bout he'd have to have it conked before anybody paid him any attention. The last thing niggers want to think about they God is that his hair kinky.

That's the truth, I say.

Ain't no way to read the bible and not think God white, she say. Then she sigh. When I found out I thought God was white, and a man, I lost interest. You mad cause he don't seem to listen to your prayers. Humph! Do the mayor listen to anything colored say? Ask Sofia. I know white people never listen to colored, period. If they do, they only listen long enough to be able to tell you what to do.

Here's the thing, say Shug. The thing I believe. God is inside you and inside everybody else. You come into the world with God. But only them that search for it inside find it. And sometimes it just manifest itself even if you not looking, or don't know what you looking for. Trouble do it for most folks, I think. Sorrow, lord. Feeling like shit.

It? I ast.

Yeah, It. God ain't a he or a she, but a It.

But what do it look like? I ast.

Don't look like nothing, she say. It ain't a picture show. It ain't something you can look at apart from anything else, including yourself. I believe God is everything, say Shug. Everything that is or ever was or ever will be. And when you can feel that, and be happy to feel that, you've found It.

Shug a beautiful something, let me tell you. She frown a little, look out cross the yard, lean back in her chair, look like a big rose.

She say, My first step from the old white man was trees. Then air. Then birds. Then other people. But one day when I was sitting quiet and feeling like a motherless child, which I was, it come to me: that feeling of being part of everything, not separate at all. I knew that if I cut a tree, my arm would bleed. And I laughed and I cried and I run all around the house. I knew just what it was. In fact, when it happen, you can't miss it. It sort of like you know what, she say, grinning and rubbing high up on my thigh.

Shug, I say.

Oh, she say. God love all them feelings. That's some of the best stuff God did. And when you know God loves 'em a lot more. You can just relax, go with everything that's going, and praise God by liking what you like.

God don't think it dirty? I ast.

Naw, she say. God made it. Listen, God love everything you love— and a mess of stuff you don't. But more than anything else, God love admiration.

You saying God vain? I ast.

Naw, she say. Not vain, just wanting to share a good thing. I think it pisses God off if you walk by the color purple in a field somewhere and don't notice it.

What it do when it pissed off? I ast.

Oh, it make something else. People think pleasing God is all God care about. But any fool living in the world can see it always trying to please us back.

Yeah? I say.

Yeah, she say. It always making little surprises and springing them on us when us least expect.

You mean it want to be loved, just like the bible say.

Yes, Celie, she say. Everything want to be loved. Us sing and dance, make faces and give flower bouquets, trying to be loved. You ever notice that trees do everything to git attention we do, except walk?

Well, us talk and talk bout God, but I'm still adrift. Trying to chase that old white man out of my head. I been so busy thinking bout him I never truly notice nothing God make. Not a blade of corn (how it do that?) not the color purple (where it come from?). Not the little wildflowers. Nothing.

Now that my eyes opening, I feels like a fool. Next to any little scrub of a bush in my yard, Mr. __'s evil sort of shrink. But not altogether. Still, it is like Shug say, You have to git man off your eyeball, before can see anything a'tall.

Man corrupt everything, say Shug. He on your box of grits, in your head, and all over the radio. He try to make you think he everywhere. Soon as you think he everywhere, you think he God. But he ain't. Whenever you trying to pray, and man plop himself on the other end of it, tell him to git lost, say Shug. Conjure up flowers, wind, water, a big rock.

But this hard work, let me tell you. He been there so long, he don't want to budge. He threaten lightening, floods and earthquakes. Us fight. I hardly pray at all. Every time I conjure up a rock, I throw it.

Amen.

Appendix B

"God's Grandeur"
by
Gerard Manley Hopkins, S.J.

The world is charged with the grandeur of God.
 It will flame out, like shining from shook foil;
 It gathers to a greatness, like the ooze of oil
Crushed, Why do men then now not reck his rod?
Generations have trod, have trod, have trod;
 And all is seared with trade; bleared, smeared with toil;
 and wears man's smudge and shares man's smell: the soil
Is bare now, nor can foot feel, being shod.

And for all this, nature is never spent;
 there lives the dearest freshness deep down things;
And though the last lights off the black West went
 Oh, morning at the brown brink eastward, springs—
Because the Holy Ghost over the bent
 World broods with warm breast and with ah! bright wings.

Appendix C

Selection from e.e. cummings

i thank You God for most this amazing
day: for the leaping greenly spirits of trees
and a blue true dream of sky; and for everything
which is natural which is infinite which is yes

(i who have died am alive again today,
and this is the sun's birthday; this is the birth
day of life and of love and wings: and of the gay
great happening illimitably earth)

how should tasting touching hearing seeing
breathing any—lifted from the no
of all nothing—human merely being
doubt unimaginable You?

(now the ears of my ears awake and
now the eyes of my eyes are opened)

Appendix D

A Summary of the Law

And behold, a certain lawyer stood up and tested Him, saying, "Teacher, what shall I do to inherit eternal life?"

He said to him, "What is written in the law? What is your reading of it?"

So he answered and said, " 'You shall love the LORD your God with all your heart, with all your soul, with all your strength, and with all your mind,' and 'your neighbor as yourself.' "

And he said to him, "You have answered rightly; do this and you will live."

But he, wanting to justify himself, said to Jesus, "And who is my neighbor?

Then Jesus answered and said: "A certain man went down from Jerusalem to Jerico, and fell among thieves, who stripped him of his clothing, wounded him, leaving him half dead.

"Now by chance a certain priest came down that road. And when he saw him, he passed by on the other side.

"Likewise a Levite, when he arrived at the place, came and looked, and passed by on the other side.

"But a certain Samaritan, as he journeyed, came where he was. And when he saw him, he had compassion on him, "and went to him and bandaged his wounds, pouring on oil and wine; and he set him on his own animal, brought him to an inn, and took care of him.

"On the next day, when he departed, he took out two denarii, gave them to the innkeeper, and said to him, 'Take care of him, and whatever more you spend, when I come again, I will repay you.'

"So which of these three do you think was neighbor to him who fell among the thieves?"

And he said, "He who showed mercy on him," Then Jesus said to him, "Go and do likewise."

Luke 10:25-37

Appendix E

The Shema

"Hear, O Israel: The LORD our God, the Lord is one!

"You shall love the LORD your God with all your heart, with all your soul, and with all your might.

"And these words which I command you today shall be in your heart;

"you shall teach them diligently to your children,
and shall talk of them when you sit in your house,
 when you walk by the way, when you lie down, and
 when you rise up.

"You shall bind them as a sign on your hand, and they shall be as frontlets between your eyes.

"You shall write them on the door posts of your house and on your gates."

Deuteronomy 6:4-9

"You shall not take vengence, nor bear any grudge against the children of your people, but
 you shall love your neighbor as yourself: I am the LORD."

Leviticus 19:18

Appendix F

Gandhi on Love

"It is no nonviolence if we merely love those
that love us. It is nonviolence only when we love
those that hate us. I know how difficult it
is to follow this grand law of love. But are not
all great and good things difficult to do? Love
of the hater is the most difficult of all. But
by the grace of God even this most difficult thing
becomes easy to accomplish if we want to do it."

"I have not been able to see any difference
between the Sermon on the Mount and the Bhagavad
Gita. What the Sermon describes in a graphic manner,
in Bhagavad Gita reduces to a scientific formula.
It may not be a scientific book in the accepted sense of the term,
but it has argued out the law of love—the law of abandon as I
would call it—
in a scientific manner."

Gandhi the Man, by Eknath Easwaran, p. 108

References

Angelou, Maya. *I Know Why the Caged Bird Sings*. New York: Bantam, 1969.

Aquinas, Thomas. *The Basic Writings of St. Thomas Aquinas*, edited by Anton C. Pegis. Vol. I and II. New York: Random House, 1945.

Auden, W.H. *Selected Poetry of W. H. Auden*. New York: Modern Library, 1959.

Belenky, Mary C., et al., *Women's Ways of Knowing*. New York: Basic Books, 1986.

The New Oxford Annotated Bible. New York: Oxford, 1977.

Chavez, Fra Angelico.

Claremont de Castillejo, Irene. *Knowing Woman*. New York: Harper Colophon, 1973.

Coles, Robert. *Dorothy Day, A Radical Devotion*. Reading: Addison-Wesley, 1987.

Cox, Harvey. *The Feast of Fools*. New York: Harper Perrennial Library, 1969.

Craven, Margaret. *I Heard the Owl Call My Name*. New York: Dell, 1973.

cummings, e.e. *100 Selected Poems by e.e. cummings*. New York: Grove Press, 1926.

Darwin, Charles. *The Origin of the Species and the Descent of Man*. New York: Modern Library, 1959.

Easwaran, Eknath. *Meditation: an Eight-Point Program*. Petaluma: Nilgiri Press, 1978.

Eliot, T.S. *Selected Poems*. London: Faber and Faber, 1954.

Erikson, Erik H. *Childhood and Society.* New York: W.W. Norton, 1963 (revised edition).

_____. *Gandhi's Truth.* New York: W.W. Norton, 1969.

_____. *Young Man Luther.* New York: W.W. Norton, 1958.

_____. *Toys and Reasons.* New York: W.W. Norton, 1977.

Farrelly, John. *God's Work in a Changing World.* Lanham: U. Press of America, 1985.

Ferlinghetti, Lawrence. *A Coney Island of the Mind.* New York: New Directions, 1958.

Fowler, James. *Stages of Faith.* New York: Harper and Row, 1981.

Frankl, Viktor. *Man's Search for Meaning.* New York: Pocket Books, 1959.

Fromm, Erich. *The Art of Loving.* New York: Bantam, 1956.

_____. *Psychoanalysis and Religion.* New York: Bantam, 1950.

Gandhi, M.K. *Selections from Gandhi,* edited by Nirmal K. Bose. Ahmedabad: Navajivan Publishing House, 1948.

Garrow, David J. *Bearing the Cross: Martin Luther King, Jr. and the Southern Leadership Conference.* New York: William Morrow, 1986.

Gilligan, Carol. *In a Different Voice.* Cambridge: Harvard U. Press, 1982.

Gross, Francis L. *How to Survive in College.* Lanham: U. Press of America, 1988.

_____. *Introducing Erik Erikson.* Lanham: U. Press of America, 1987.

_____. *Passages in Teaching.* New York: Philosophical Library, 1982.

Hick, John. *Death and Eternal Life.* New York: Harper and Row, 1984.

Hopkins, Gerard Manley. *Poems and Prose of Gerard Manley Hopkins*, selected by W.H. Gardner. Baltimore: Penguin Books, 1953.

James, William. *The Varieties of Religious Experience*. New York, Modern Library, 1902.

John of the Cross (See also Juan de la Cruz). *The Collected Writings of John of the Cross* translated by Kieran Kavanaugh and Otilio Rodriguez. Washington: ICS Publications, 1979.

Jung, C.G. *The Basic Writings of C.G. Jung*. New York: Modern Library, 1959.

_____. *Memories, Dreams, and Reflections*. New York: Vantage Books, 1961.

_____. *Psychology and Religion*. Cambridge: Yale U. Press, 1961.

Kegan, Robert. *The Evolving Self*. Cambridge: Harvard U. Press, 1982.

King, Coretta Scott. *My Life with Martin Luther King, Jr.* New York: Holt, Rinehard, Winston, 1969.

King, Martin Luther, Jr. *Why We Can't Wait*. New York: Mentor Books, 1963.

Kohlberg, Lawrence. *The Philosophy of Moral Development, Volume One*. New York: Harper and Row, 1981.

Kung, Hans. *Eternal Life?* Garden City: Doubleday, 1984.

Leguin, Ursula K. *A Wizard of Earthsea*. New York: Bantam, 1968.

Leon-Dufour, Xavier (ed.) *Vocabulaire de Theologie Biblique*. Paris: Editions du Cerf, 1964.

Loyola, Ignatius. *The Text of the Spriitual Exercises of St. Ignatius*. Westminster: Newman Press, 1949.

Marshall, Eric, and Hemple, Scott (eds.). *Children's Letters to God*. New York: Simon and Schuster, 1966.

Marx, Karl, and Engels, Friedrich. *The Communist Manifesto.* New York: Washington Square, 1964.

Marx, Karl, *Critique of Hegel's Philosophy of Right.* Cambridge: Cambridge University Press, 1970.

Nemeck, Francis Kelley, and Coombs, Marie Theresa. *Comtemplation.* Wilmington: William Glazier, 1982.

_____. *The Spritual Journey.* Wilmington: William Glazier, 1987.

Peguy, Charles. *Basic Verities,* translated by Anne and Julian Greene. Chicago: Logos Books, 1943.

_____. *God Speaks,* translated by Julian Greene. New York: Pantheon, 1945.

Perry, William G., Jr. *Forms of Intellectual and Ethical Development in the College Years.* New York: Holt, Rinehart, Winston, 1968.

Pieper, Joseph. *Leisure: the Basis of Culture.* New York: Pantheon, 1962.

Sagan, Carl. *Contact.* New York: Simon and Schuster, 1985.

Smith, Erwin. *The Ethics of Martin Luther King, Jr.,* New York: Edwin Mellin Press, 1981.

Smith, Gibbs, M. *Joe Hill.* Salt Lake City: U. of Utah Press, 1969.

Tandon, Prakash. *Punjabi Century.* Berkeley: U. of California Press, 1961.

Teilhard de Chardin, Pierre. *The Divine Milieu.* New York: Harper and Row, 1968.

Teresa of Avila, *The Collected Works of Teresa of Avila* translated by Kieran Kavanaugh and Otilio Rodriguez. Washington: ICA Publications, 1976-85.

Thoreau, Henry David. *Walden.* New York: Modern Library, 1937.

Walker, Alice. *The Color Purple.* New York: Harcourt, Brace, Jovanovich, 1982.